Great Sedona Hikes

A HIKING GUIDE CONTAINING INFORMATION
ON THE 50 GREATEST TRAILS
IN SEDONA, ARIZONA

D1409327

by

William Bohan

and

David Butler

Nonliability Statement

The authors have taken every precaution to ensure that the information contained within is up-to-date, accurate and reflects trail conditions when this guide was published. However, trail conditions frequently change because of weather, Forest Service activity or other causes. The GPS data included were obtained from a GPSmap76S Garmin GPS unit. Because the data are only as accurate as the sensitivity of the GPS unit, some inaccuracies may be present. Users of GPS data are urged to use common sense when hiking. Always stay on the trail. The authors, publisher, contributors, and all those involved in the preparation of this book, either directly or indirectly, disclaim any liability for injuries, accidents, and damages whatsoever that may occur to those using this book. You are responsible for your health and safety while hiking the trails.

Table of Contents

About the Authors

This guide is a result of a collaboration between William Bohan and David Butler, two avid Sedona hikers.

William (Bill) was born in Michigan and spent his entire working life there. Following retirement from a major auto company in 2001 as an Executive Engineer, he moved to Sedona in 2002 and began hiking shortly thereafter. On these hikes he took numerous photos and, in 2005, started the Great Sedona Hikes website (http://greatsedonahikes.com) as a way to easily share the photos with his fellow hikers. Bill continues to hike the trails in Sedona and updates the information on his website on a regular basis.

David was born in Ohio and was Associate Dean of the College of the Arts at a major Ohio university until he retired in 2003. After moving to Sedona, he began hiking with a local hiking group. He is an enthusiastic photographer, who has hiked over 100 trails in the area with his wife Ruth.

This guidebook includes the greatest 50 hikes in Sedona, as rated by Bill and David. They have hiked most of the trails in the Sedona area and each author has a broad-based wealth of hiking experience. There are other trails available in the Sedona area, but the ones included in this book are simply the Great Sedona Hikes.

If you have suggestions or comments on the guidebook, email Bill and David at: hikebook@greatsedonahikes.com

Acknowledgments

The authors would like to acknowledge several individuals for their contributions to this book. They are:
Our wives, Nancy Williams and Ruth Butler for their efforts in editing this work; René and Michele Braun, Lou Camp, Mary Heyborne, Helen Mueller, Roberta Petersen, Tom and Becky Solon, Darryl and Lorna Thompson, Charlie and Marilyn Weaver, and Jerry York for their companionship while hiking the trails.

Hiking Tips

The stunning red rock formations, moderate temperatures and close proximity to the trails make hiking in Sedona an experience unlike anywhere else in the world, but hiking is not without risk.

It is very important to be prepared, even for a day hike. The atmosphere is very dry in Sedona so bring enough water to stay hydrated and drink water throughout the hike. In addition:

- Wear a hat and sunscreen
- Wear hiking boots or good walking shoes, as the trails can be uneven and rocky
- In your pack carry a first-aid kit, a fully charged cell phone (although many hiking trails do not have cell phone service), flashlight, compass, map, portable GPS unit, rescue whistle, pocketknife and a snack
- Trailhead parking lots can be the target of thieves so don't leave valuables in your vehicle
- Check the weather before you begin hiking, and reschedule your hike if inclement weather is predicted
- Let someone know where you'll be hiking, hike with at least one other person and complete your hike before sunset
- Downhill hikers have the right-of-way in most instances because footing is more tenuous downhill than uphill. If hiking uphill, step aside and let downhill hikers pass
- Bicyclists are supposed to yield to all trail users, but use common sense and step aside if appropriate
- Remember, hiking is not a race. Slow down and look around while hiking; many times the best views are behind you

Required Parking Pass

When you park on the National Forest around Sedona, you'll need a Red Rock Pass or its equivalent. If you park on private property (not National Forest land), you do not need a Red Rock Pass (or equivalent). Nor do you need one if you are going to be driving around enjoying the scenery, stopping to take a photo, or parking and remaining near your vehicle.

The Red Rock Pass program began several years ago to support the National Forest area around Sedona. The Forest Service uses the funds raised through this program for trail development and maintenance. The Red Rock Pass is available as a Daily Pass for $5 per day, a Weekly Pass for $15, or an Annual Pass for $20.

- The Daily Pass permits you to park on the National Forest for the day of issue. It expires at midnight. It does not include the parking fees at 4 fee areas: Crescent Moon Ranch/Red Rock Crossing ($10), West Fork Trail ($10), Grasshopper Point Picnic Area ($8), and Banjo Bill Picnic Area ($8). The parking fee for each area is separate (each area charges separately).

- The Weekly Pass permits you to park on the National Forest for 7 days and includes the additional parking fees at the 4 fee areas.

- The $20 Annual Pass permits you to park on the National Forest for 1 year. It does not include the parking fees at the 4 fee areas.

Instead of a Red Rock Pass, you may display any of the following equivalents: 1) a National Parks Pass, also known as a Federal Interagency Annual Pass ($80); 2) a Senior Pass, also known as a Federal Interagency Senior Pass, issued to U.S. residents 62 years of age and older (one-time $10 cost); or 3) a Federal Interagency Access Pass, issued to individuals with permanent disabilities (no cost). If you show either pass 2) or 3) at any of the 4 fee areas, you'll receive a discount of 50% off the parking fees.

Sedona Average Weather & Sunrise-Sunset Data

	Temperature F Daily High	Daily Low	Precipitation (Inches)	Sunrise	Sunset
				(1st of Month)	
January	56	30	2.10	7:32 AM	5:30 PM
February	60	33	2.16	7:24 AM	5:58 PM
March	65	37	2.47	6:57 AM	6:24 PM
April	73	42	1.16	6:16 AM	6:48 PM
May	82	49	0.71	5:40 AM	7:10 PM
June	93	58	0.36	5:19 AM	7:32 PM
July	97	64	1.65	5:21 AM	7:42 PM
August	94	63	1.90	5:40 AM	7:29 PM
September	88	58	1.94	6:02 AM	6:55 PM
October	77	48	1.67	6:22 AM	6:14 PM
November	64	36	1.38	6:46 AM	5:37 PM
December	57	31	1.51	7:14 AM	5:20 PM
Average	75	46	1.50		

Vortex Information

The Sedona vortex experience is unique. Some describe vortexes as places where energy flows in or out of the earth, with masculine and/or feminine, electrical and/or magnetic properties. There are four main vortexes: Airport Mesa Vortex, Bell Rock Vortex, Boynton Canyon Vortex, and Cathedral Rock Vortex. All locations are described in this guidebook. We suggest that you approach each vortex with no preconceived ideas of what you may experience, and just let the experience "happen." If nothing else, you'll enjoy some of Sedona's finest views.

GPS Data

When you read the hike descriptions, you will find numbers in curly brackets such as {1}, {2}, and so on. These numbers refer to the GPS checkpoints in the maps below each of the hike descriptions. Also see the detailed descriptions of the GPS checkpoints beginning on page 114. Specific GPS data in the universal .gpx format for all the hikes contained in this guidebook (plus many additional hikes) are available at: http://greatsedonahikes.com/gps/gps.html.

Definition of the "Y"

If you obtain directions from a Sedona local, chances are he or she will give you those directions referencing something called the "Y." We use the "Y" as our reference point in this guidebook also. Some history is in order.

Before the age of roundabouts (traffic circles), there was a traffic light at the intersection of State Route 89A and State Route 179. If you could look at that intersection with a bird's eye view, it would have looked like an elongated letter "Y." And that is why locals refer to that intersection as "the Y."

The traffic light at State Routes 89A and 179 has been replaced by two roundabouts so the intersection is really no longer in the shape of a "Y" but the reference continues. So, if you come to Sedona by driving north on SR 179, the "Y" is the northern end of SR 179.

If you drive to Sedona from Flagstaff on SR 89A, the "Y" is the first of the two roundabouts you come to. And, if you drive to Sedona from Cottonwood, the "Y" is the second roundabout you enter, which is very close to the first roundabout.

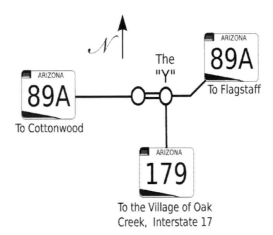

Alphabetical List of Included Hikes

Master Hike Locator

Oak Creek Canyon Hikes

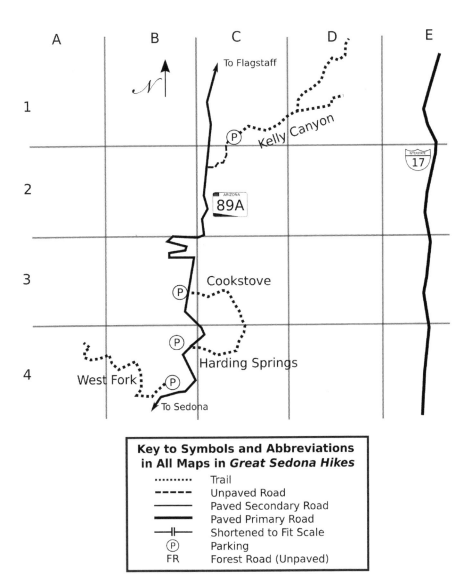

To Flagstaff

Kelly Canyon

89A

Cookstove

Harding Springs

West Fork

To Sedona

Key to Symbols and Abbreviations in All Maps in *Great Sedona Hikes*

··········	Trail
------	Unpaved Road
———	Paved Secondary Road
▬▬▬	Paved Primary Road
─╫─	Shortened to Fit Scale
Ⓟ	Parking
FR	Forest Road (Unpaved)

Master Hike Locator

Sedona Hikes (North)

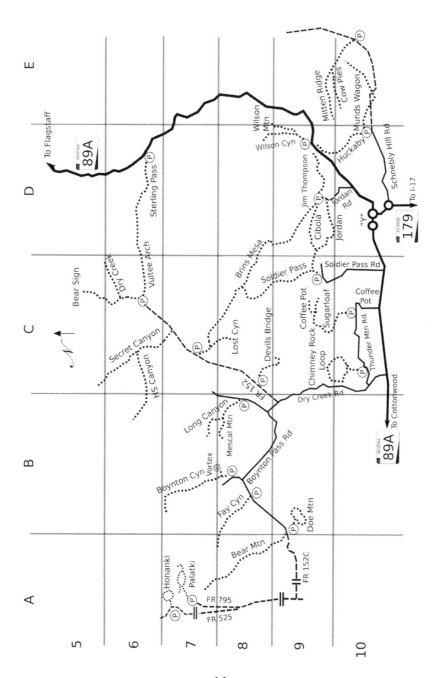

Master Hike Locator

Sedona Hikes (South)

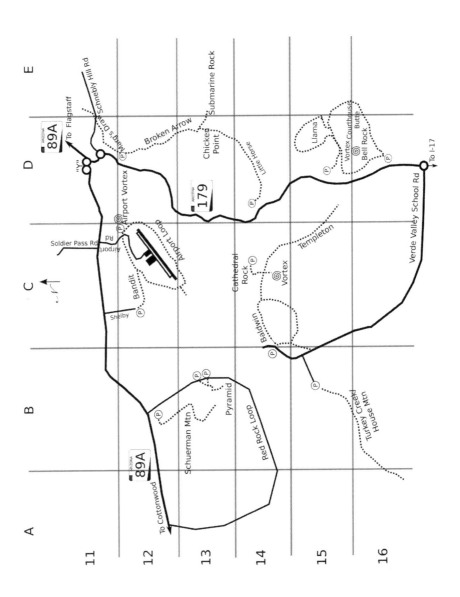

Master Hike Locator

Hikes South of the Village of Oak Creek

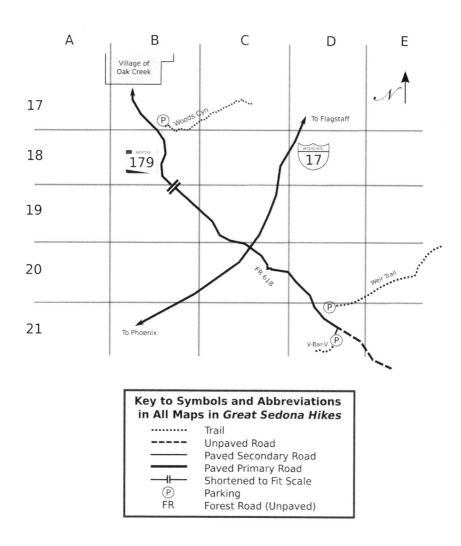

Village of Oak Creek

A   B   C   D   E

17

18

19

20

21

Woods Cyn

To Flagstaff

ARIZONA
179

INTERSTATE
17

FR 618

Weir Trail

To Phoenix

V-Bar-V

**Key to Symbols and Abbreviations
in All Maps in *Great Sedona Hikes***

....	Trail
- - - -	Unpaved Road
————	Paved Secondary Road
▬▬▬▬	Paved Primary Road
—⫠⫠—	Shortened to Fit Scale
Ⓟ	Parking
FR	Forest Road (Unpaved)

Airport Loop Trail

Summary: A loop hike that circles the Sedona Airport with nice views all around

Challenge Level: Easy to Moderate

Hiking Distance: About 4 miles total, but add another 0.8 miles if you hike the Tabletop Trail

Trailhead Directions: There are two ways to access this trail. From the "Y" roundabout (the intersection of State Route 89A and State Route 179), drive west toward Cottonwood for 1.0 mile and then turn left on Airport Road. The primary trailhead is located approximately 0.5 mile up Airport Road on the left at GPS coordinates: 34° 51.345' North; 111° 46.804' West {2}. There is parking for about a dozen vehicles here.

A secondary trailhead is located on Shelby Drive {1}, for the Bandit Trail. Shelby Drive is approximately 1.5 miles west of the "Y." Turn left (south) on Shelby Drive. Just past the Sedona Recycles building, Shelby turns left. The parking is on the right. Hike the Bandit Trail until it intersects the Airport Loop Trail. Continue in a clockwise direction on the Airport Loop Trail. Using the Bandit Trail to get to the Airport Loop Trail {5}, will add about 0.8 mile to your hike.

Description: As you hike around Airport Mesa below the Sedona Airport, there are good views all around. The sun on the south side of this circular hike makes photographs a challenge. On the east, there are great views of Twin Buttes and, from the south, Cathedral Rock. Be sure to hike the Tabletop Trail at the south end of the runway, GPS coordinates: 34° 50.773' N; 111° 47.724' W {3}. Follow Tabletop about 0.4 mile to the end of the mesa {4}, and then back. This hike provides nice views of Chimney Rock, Capital Butte and Coffeepot Rock on the north side of the loop.

Note: The Airport Loop Trail is very rocky in places and there are steep drop-offs on the south side of Airport Mesa. Don't attempt this hike if a narrow trail and steep drop-offs are a concern.

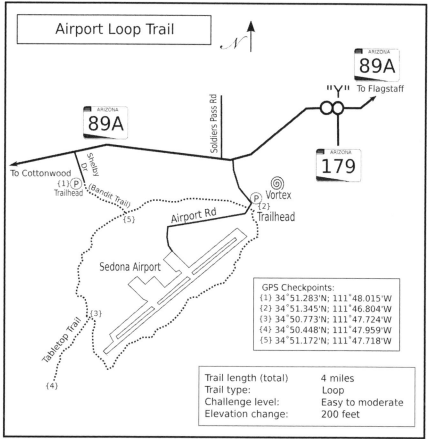

Airport Loop Trail

GPS Checkpoints:
{1} 34°51.283'N; 111°48.015'W
{2} 34°51.345'N; 111°46.804'W
{3} 34°50.773'N; 111°47.724'W
{4} 34°50.448'N; 111°47.959'W
{5} 34°51.172'N; 111°47.718'W

Trail length (total)	4 miles
Trail type:	Loop
Challenge level:	Easy to moderate
Elevation change:	200 feet

Airport Vortex Trail

Summary: Not a hike so much as it is a bit of an in-and-out scramble to the vortex located on Airport Mesa

Challenge Level: Easy in distance, but you need to hike up a steep trail

Hiking Distance: Less than 0.25 mile round trip

Trailhead Directions: From the "Y" roundabout (the intersection of State Route 89A and State Route 179), drive west toward Cottonwood for 1.0 mile and then turn left on Airport Road. The trailhead is located approximately 0.5 mile up Airport Road on the left at GPS coordinates: 34° 51.345' North; 111° 46.804' West {1}. There is parking for about a dozen vehicles here.

Description: From the parking area on Airport Road, you'll see a red rock formation to the left and Airport Mesa to the right. Follow the main trail east toward the rock until you come to a sign for the overlook in about 200 feet. Turn left {2} and follow the trail that leads to "The Overlook". The top of the rock formation is considered to be the vortex {4}.

Baldwin Trail

Summary: This loop trail at the base of Cathedral Rock offers some excellent views and a short side trip to the banks of Oak Creek

Challenge Level: Moderate

Hiking Distance: About a 3.3 mile loop.

Trailhead Directions: The trailhead is located on the unpaved portion of Verde Valley School Road. From the "Y" roundabout (the intersection of State Route 89A and State Route 179), drive south on SR 179 for 7 miles to the SR 179, Jack's Canyon and Verde Valley School Road roundabout and then turn right (west). Drive approximately 4.5 miles west on Verde Valley School Road to the parking area on the left (south) side of the road at GPS coordinates: 34° 49.309' North; 111° 48.493' West {1}. The trailhead is across the road.

Description: This hike, which circles a red rock butte beside Cathedral Rock, provides excellent panoramic views of Cathedral

18

Rock. After crossing the road, you'll come to a signboard {2}. You can hike in either direction. If you hike in the clockwise direction, you'll intersect the Templeton Trail after 0.5 mile {4}. Take a side trip on Templeton and hike towards Oak Creek. After 0.2 mile, look across the creek to see "Buddha Beach," where visitors use river rock to build amazing stacked structures {5}. Periodically, floods knock the structures down, but they are usually quickly replaced. You may be lucky and see hundreds of "buddhas." Return to the Baldwin Trail and then continue around the tall red rock butte. You'll pass some excellent places to stop and enjoy the views {6} {7} on your loop. We hike in the morning so the views of Cathedral Rock are somewhat obscured by looking into the sun. It might be better to make this hike later in the day to get pictures of Cathedral Rock.

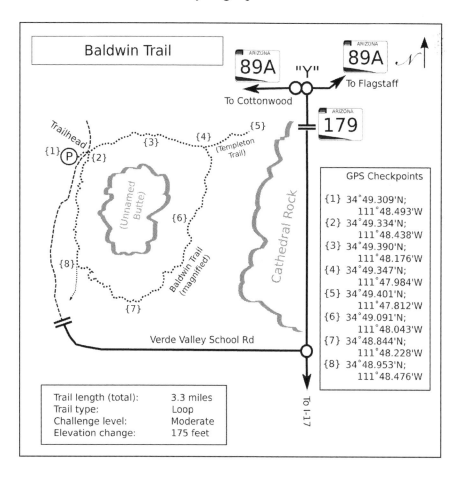

Trail length (total):	3.3 miles
Trail type:	Loop
Challenge level:	Moderate
Elevation change:	175 feet

GPS Checkpoints

{1} 34°49.309'N; 111°48.493'W
{2} 34°49.334'N; 111°48.438'W
{3} 34°49.390'N; 111°48.176'W
{4} 34°49.347'N; 111°47.984'W
{5} 34°49.401'N; 111°47.812'W
{6} 34°49.091'N; 111°48.043'W
{7} 34°48.844'N; 111°48.228'W
{8} 34°48.953'N; 111°48.476'W

Bear Mountain Trail

Summary: A strenuous, sunny, in-and-out hike with excellent red rock views

Challenge Level: Hard

Hiking Distance: To the top of Bear Mountain is about 2.5 miles each way; 5 miles round trip

Trailhead Directions: The parking for Bear Mountain hike is shared with the Doe Mountain trail. From the "Y" roundabout (the intersection of State Route 89A and State Route 179), drive west toward Cottonwood on SR 89A about 3 miles. Turn right on Dry Creek Road (where speed limits are strictly enforced). Stay on Dry Creek to a stop sign (about 3 miles) and then turn left on Boynton Pass Road. Proceed about 1.5 miles to a stop sign. Turn left, continuing on Boynton Pass Road. The trailhead parking is the second area on the left side, about 1.75 miles from the stop sign. The GPS coordinates for the parking lot are: 34° 53.596' North; 111°

51.945' West {1}. The trailhead is across the road from the parking area.

Description: Bear Mountain provides fantastic views of Doe Mountain (and beyond), and nearby canyons. Climbing from about 4500 feet at the parking lot/trailhead, there is a natural stopping place and photo opportunity at elevation 5500 feet {2}. The total elevation gain to the top is some 1800 feet. From the top of Bear Mountain {3}, you can see the San Francisco Peaks in Flagstaff. Note: there are some exposed and extreme drop-offs on parts of this trail – watch your footing.

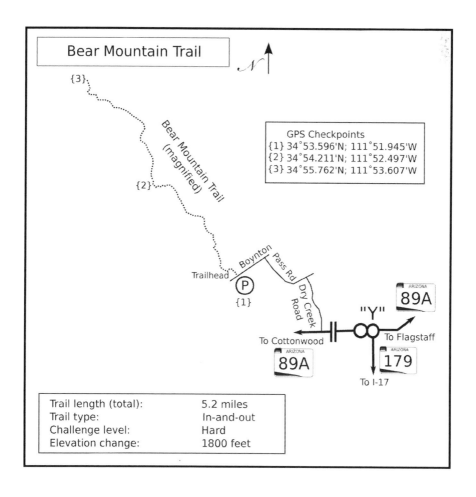

GPS Checkpoints
{1} 34°53.596'N; 111°51.945'W
{2} 34°54.211'N; 111°52.497'W
{3} 34°55.762'N; 111°53.607'W

Trail length (total):	5.2 miles
Trail type:	In-and-out
Challenge level:	Hard
Elevation change:	1800 feet

Bear Sign Trail

Summary: A beautiful, solitary in-and-out hike in a forested red rock canyon

Challenge Level: Moderate

Hiking Distance: About 3 miles each way; 6 miles round trip

Trailhead Directions: From the "Y" roundabout (the intersection of State Route 89A and State Route 179), drive west toward Cottonwood on SR 89A for 3 miles. Turn right on Dry Creek Road (where speed limits are strictly enforced). Stay on Dry Creek for 2 miles and then turn right on Forest Road (FR) 152. Proceed to the end of FR 152 (about 4.5 miles) to the parking area on the left at GPS coordinates 34° 56.236' North; 111° 47.678' West {1}. NOTE: FR 152 can be an extremely rough road so a high clearance vehicle is recommended. The parking area is the same as used for the Dry Creek and Vultee Arch trails.

Description: After you park, proceed in a northwesterly direction on the Dry Creek Trail. You'll be hiking in the forest so there is shade. The trail is relatively flat. After about 0.6 mile, you'll come to a fork where the Dry Creek Trail goes to the right and the Bear Sign Trail begins to the left at GPS coordinates 34° 56.723' N; 111° 47.680' W {2}. You'll hike among some large Manzanita trees, unusual because most of the Manzanita are bushes around Sedona. You may actually see signs of bear along the trail – we have! Hike some 2.8 miles to the intersection of the David Miller Trail at GPS coordinates 34° 57.656' N; 111° 49.054' W {3}. A short, but steep hike up the David Miller Trail about 0.2 mile provides a lovely view from the saddle of the ridge between Bear Sign and Secret Canyons {4}.

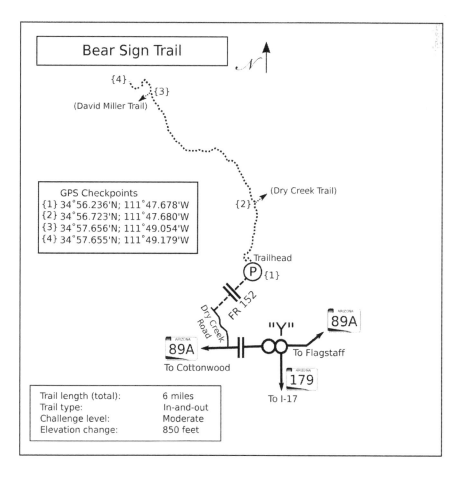

GPS Checkpoints		
{1} 34°56.236'N; 111°47.678'W		
{2} 34°56.723'N; 111°47.680'W		
{3} 34°57.656'N; 111°49.054'W		
{4} 34°57.655'N; 111°49.179'W		

Trail length (total):	6 miles
Trail type:	In-and-out
Challenge level:	Moderate
Elevation change:	850 feet

23

Bell Rock Vortex

Summary: Explore the north side of Bell Rock on this in-and-out hike, where you may experience some vortex energy

Challenge Level: Easy to Moderate

Hiking Distance: About 0.5 mile each way; 1 mile round trip to Bell Rock: you can double this distance if you explore Bell Rock

Trailhead Directions: From the "Y" roundabout (the intersection of State Route 89A and State Route 179), drive south on State Route 179 for about 8 miles. The trailhead parking area is just north of Bell Rock at GPS coordinates: 34° 48.350' North; 111° 46.009' West {1}. There are toilets at the parking area. The trail starts on the southeast side of the parking area on the opposite side from the toilets.

Description: The south side of Bell Rock is too steep to hike, so you'll be parking and hiking on the north side. From the north

24

parking area, you begin hiking 0.2 mile south on a connecting trail that parallels SR 179 on your right. When you reach the intersection of the Bell Rock and the Courthouse Butte Trails {2} continue straight ahead toward Bell Rock {3} and then follow the cairns for the Bell Rock Trail. Hike for 0.1 mile and then make a right turn {4} on the large flat rocks. Hike around to the east and climb up on the rocks to a wonderful meditation perch {5}. Take some time to do some additional exploration of Bell Rock. People have reported feeling vortex energy at many places on Bell Rock; so explore it to find that place where you feel the energy. But as you climb on Bell Rock, watch your footing. The rock can be very slippery, particularly if it is wet.

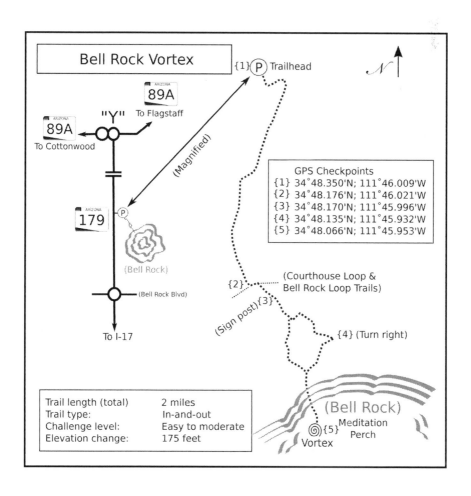

Boynton Canyon Trail

Summary: An in-and-out hike of a forested canyon with nice red rock views

Challenge Level: Moderate

Hiking Distance: About 3 miles each way; 6 miles round trip

Trailhead Directions: From the "Y" roundabout (the intersection of State Route 89A and State Route 179), drive west on SR 89A toward Cottonwood about 3 miles. Turn right on Dry Creek Road (where speed limits are strictly enforced). Stay on Dry Creek to a stop sign (about 3 miles) and then turn left on Boynton Pass Road. Proceed about 1.5 miles to a stop sign. Turn right, the trailhead parking is about 0.1 mile on the right at GPS coordinates 34° 54.456' North; 111° 50.928' West {1}. There are toilets at the parking area.

Description: Located beyond the Enchantment Resort, Boynton Canyon is a very popular hike. We like it for its summer shade, good red rock views and vortex energy. After hiking about 0.25 mile from the parking lot, you'll see a sign for the Boynton Vista Trail to the right at GPS coordinates: 34° 54.623' N; 111° 50.987' W {2}. Hike the Vista trail for about 0.38 mile slightly uphill to two tall rock formations, both of which are considered vortex points {3}. After your vortex experience, return to the Boynton Canyon Trail and then continue to the right. Once you are past the Enchantment Resort, you can see evidence of prior habitation on the right {4}. Soon you'll enter a forest where the trail and views are excellent. You'll see some nice fall colors during the third week of October. The trail ends in a box canyon at the base of Secret Mountain {5}.

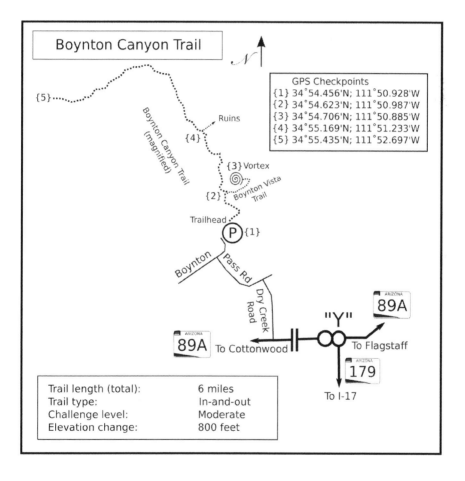

Brins Mesa Trail

Summary: An in-and-out hike to the top of a beautiful mesa with red rock views all around

Challenge Level: Moderate

Hiking Distance: This hike has two trailheads, one located in-town and the second off Forest Road (FR) 152. From the in-town trailhead, you'll hike 1.4 miles one way to the mesa top. If you hike west and down to the second trailhead, you'll hike another 2.4 miles for a total round trip of 7.5 miles. Another option at the mesa top is to hike east about 0.5 mile to a red rock knoll for a spectacular view overlooking Mormon Canyon

Trailhead Directions: To access the in-town trailhead, from the "Y" roundabout (the intersection of State Route 89A and State Route 179), drive north on SR 89A to Jordan Road. Turn left on Jordan Road then drive to the end. Turn left on Park Ridge Drive and then proceed through the paved cul de sac, continuing on the dirt road for 0.5 mile. The parking area is located at GPS coordinates: 34° 53.287' North; 111° 46.098' West {1}. There are toilets at the parking area.
To access the second trailhead off FR 152, from the "Y" roundabout, drive west on SR 89A toward Cottonwood for 3 miles. Turn right on to Dry Creek Road (where speed limits are strictly enforced). Drive

for 2 miles and then turn right on FR 152. Proceed for 2.5 miles to the parking area on your right at GPS coordinates: 34° 55.008' N; 111° 48.525' W {4}. NOTE: FR 152 can be extremely rough so a high clearance vehicle is recommended.

Description: Hiking from the in-town trailhead provides some outstanding views. The trail becomes steeper as you approach the mesa. Once you reach the mesa {2} , you'll enjoy views all around. Turn right to go to the Mormon Canyon overlook. Turn left to hike to the second trailhead on FR 152. In about 1 mile you'll intersect the Soldier Pass Trail {3}.

Hiking from the trailhead on FR 152 is a pleasant, moderate uphill hike through trees. If possible, you may want to do this hike with two vehicles, one parked at each trailhead.

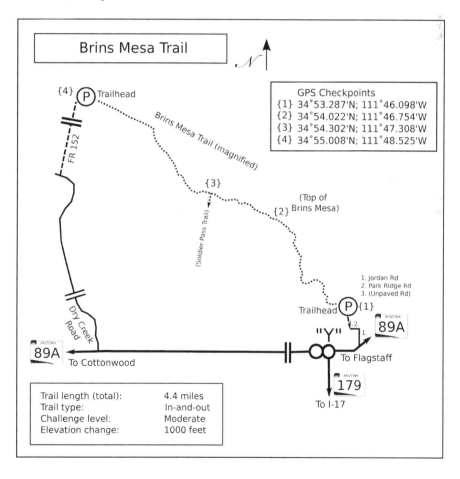

Brins Mesa Trail

GPS Checkpoints
{1} 34°53.287'N; 111°46.098'W
{2} 34°54.022'N; 111°46.754'W
{3} 34°54.302'N; 111°47.308'W
{4} 34°55.008'N; 111°48.525'W

Trailhead
FR 152
Brins Mesa Trail (magnified)
(Soldier Pass Trail)
(Top of Brins Mesa)
1. Jordan Rd
2. Park Ridge Rd
3. (Unpaved Rd)
Trailhead
"Y"
ARIZONA 89A
Dry Creek Road
ARIZONA 89A
To Cottonwood
To Flagstaff
ARIZONA 179
To I-17

Trail length (total):	4.4 miles
Trail type:	In-and-out
Challenge level:	Moderate
Elevation change:	1000 feet

below

Broken Arrow Trail

Summary: A sunny, in-and-out trip to Devil's Dining Room, Submarine Rock and Chicken Point with great red rock views

Challenge Level: Moderate

Hiking Distance: About 1.5 miles each way; 3 miles round trip but add another 1.3 miles if you hike to Submarine Rock

Trailhead Directions: From the "Y" roundabout (the intersection of State Route 89A and State Route 179), drive south on SR 179 1.5 miles to the roundabout at Morgan Road. Turn left (east) on Morgan Road and then drive about 0.6 mile to the trailhead parking on your left at GPS coordinates 34° 50.738' North; 111° 45.424' West {1}.

Description: From the parking area, go across the jeep road to the trail. Initially, the trail essentially parallels the jeep road. After hiking about 0.5 mile, you'll come to a sinkhole known as the Devil's

30

Dining Room on the left {2}. As you continue along the trail, after about 1 mile you'll come to a fork in the trail {3}. Go left to Submarine Rock. While both ends can be climbed, the north "tower" is a bit steep so go around to the south end for nice views from on top {4}. Retrace your steps to the fork in the trail and then turn left (south) to proceed to Chicken Point, named for thrill-seeking jeep drivers who once dared to drive close to the edge of the point. Jeep access is no longer permitted on Chicken Point. From here the panoramic red rock views are wonderful {5}.

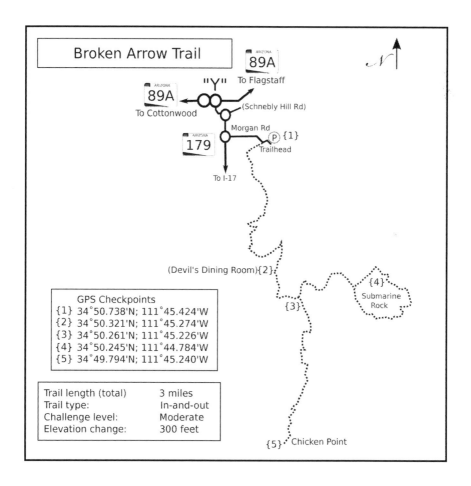

Broken Arrow Trail

89A

"Y"   To Flagstaff

89A

(Schnebly Hill Rd)

To Cottonwood

Morgan Rd

179

(P) {1}
Trailhead

To I-17

(Devil's Dining Room){2}

{4}

Submarine Rock

{3}

GPS Checkpoints
{1} 34°50.738'N; 111°45.424'W
{2} 34°50.321'N; 111°45.274'W
{3} 34°50.261'N; 111°45.226'W
{4} 34°50.245'N; 111°44.784'W
{5} 34°49.794'N; 111°45.240'W

Trail length (total)	3 miles
Trail type:	In-and-out
Challenge level:	Moderate
Elevation change:	300 feet

{5} Chicken Point

Cathedral Rock Trail

Summary: A steep, sunny in-and-out hike to the "saddle" of Cathedral Rock for spectacular views all around

Challenge Level: Hard

Hiking Distance: About 0.75 miles each way; 1.5 miles round trip

Trailhead Directions: From the "Y" roundabout (the intersection of State Route 89A and State Route 179), drive south on SR 179 for 3.2 miles to the Back 'O Beyond roundabout. Go west on the Back 'O Beyond Road for about 0.75 mile. The parking area is on your left at GPS coordinates 34° 49.523' North; 111° 47.303' West {1}.

Description: If you want to get up close and personal with Cathedral Rock, this short, strenuous hike is for you. The trail begins on the right (west) side of the parking area. You'll start out crossing a dry creek bed. Continue climbing up until the trail intersects the Templeton Trail {2}. Turn right and then go about 60 paces to the branching off of the Cathedral Rock Trail on your left {3}. From here the trail climbs steeply. Good hiking boots are recommended. Once you are in the saddle {4}, you are at the location of one of four main vortex sites in Sedona. There are short trails along the south side of the east and west rock formations that lead to some good views, although the footing can be tricky. Note: If heights or tenuous footing bothers you, we do not recommend this trail.

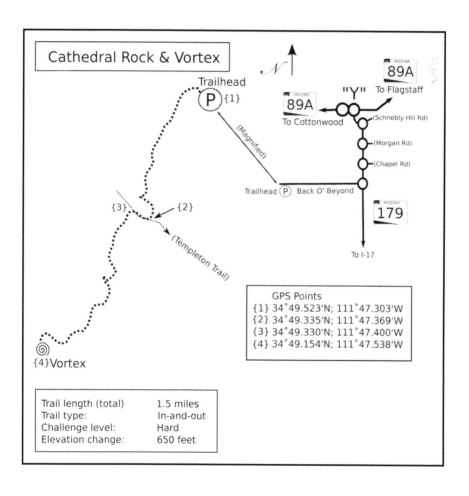

Cathedral Rock & Vortex		

Trailhead

(P) {1}

89A
To Cottonwood

"Y" To Flagstaff

89A

(Schnebly Hill Rd)

(Morgan Rd)

(Chapel Rd)

(Magnified)

Trailhead (P) Back O' Beyond

179

{3} {2}

(Templeton Trail)

To I-17

GPS Points
{1} 34°49.523'N; 111°47.303'W
{2} 34°49.335'N; 111°47.369'W
{3} 34°49.330'N; 111°47.400'W
{4} 34°49.154'N; 111°47.538'W

{4}Vortex

Trail length (total)	1.5 miles
Trail type:	In-and-out
Challenge level:	Hard
Elevation change:	650 feet

Chimney Rock Loop Trail

Summary: A loop hike around the base of Chimney Rock with panoramic views

Challenge Level: Moderate

Hiking Distance: About 2.25 miles round trip

Trailhead Directions: From the "Y" roundabout (the intersection of State Route 89A and State Route 179), drive west toward Cottonwood on SR 89A for 3 miles to Dry Creek Road (where speed limits are strictly enforced). Turn right on Dry Creek Road and then proceed for 0.7 mile. Turn right on Thunder Mountain Road and then drive 0.6 mile. The parking area is on your left at GPS coordinates: 34° 52.325' North; 111° 48.735' West {1}. The entrance gate opens each day at 8:00 am; the exit gate is never closed.

Description: From the parking area, go west on the trail for about 100 feet and then turn right on the Thunder Mountain Trail. In 0.1 miles you'll come to the intersection of Thunder Mountain and

Chimney Rock Trails {2}. Turn right here. We prefer to hike around the base of Chimney Rock in the counterclockwise direction because the steep trail on the northeast side is easier (and safer) to hike uphill versus going downhill. As you circle Chimney Rock, you'll have panoramic views of the mountains around Sedona and you'll intersect the Andante {3}, Lizard Head {8}, and Lower Chimney Trails {10}. At the 0.8 mile mark, you'll see a fencepost on your right {5}. About 50 feet past the fencepost, the more adventurous can turn right to take a short, steep side trail up to an overlook {6}; it's a scramble but worth it for the view. About 180 feet past the fencepost is another unmarked trail {7} to the left, another scramble, which leads to the "chimney" of Chimney Rock. Continuing on, at 1.4 miles you'll intersect a steep trail, which leads to the summit on Little Sugarloaf {10}; stay left to complete the Chimney Rock Loop.

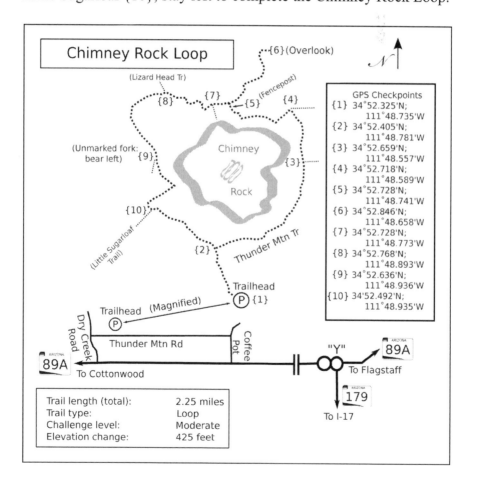

Cibola Pass Trail

Summary: This close-to-town, in-and-out hike provides some spectacular red rock views

Challenge Level: Moderate

Hiking Distance: About 0.8 mile each way; 1.6 miles round trip if you hike the Cibola Trail in-and-out. About 2 miles round trip, if you hike the Cibola Pass Trail then return to the parking area via the Jordan Trail. If you continue west on the Jordan Trail to the Soldier Pass Trail and then continue on to the Seven Sacred Pools, passing Devil's Kitchen, you'll add about 2 miles, making the total round trip distance 4 miles.

Trailhead Directions: From the "Y" roundabout (the intersection of State Route 89A and State Route 179), drive north on SR 89A to Jordan Road. Turn left on Jordan Road and then drive to the end. Turn left on Park Ridge Drive and then proceed through the paved cul de sac, continuing on the dirt road for 0.5 mile. The parking area is located at GPS coordinates: 34° 53.287' North; 111° 46.098' West {1}. There are toilets at the parking area.

Description: The Cibola Pass trail branches left from the Brins Mesa trail at GPS coordinates 34° 53.281' N; 111° 46.138' W {2}. The trail has places where it is quite steep. As you proceed, you'll have some very nice red rock views. At about 0.6 mile, you'll approach two posts on the left side {3}. If you go straight for a short distance, you'll have some great views. Return to the posts and then continue on the trail. You'll meet the Jordan Trail after hiking 0.8 mile {4}. Turn around here to return to the parking area. Or proceed west on the Jordan Trail to the Soldier Pass Trail. Turn right on the Soldier Pass Trail, which leads to Devil's Kitchen (a very large sink hole) {5} and then on to the Seven Sacred Pools {6}. From the Seven Pools, you'll have hiked about 4 miles when you return to the parking area via the Jordan Trail.

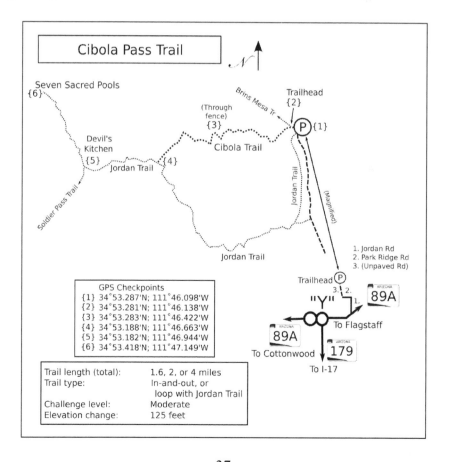

Coffeepot Trail

Summary: An in-town, in-and-out trail that takes you to the base of Coffeepot Rock

Challenge Level: Easy

Hiking Distance: About 1.2 miles each way; 2.4 miles round trip

Trailhead Directions: From the "Y" roundabout (the intersection of State Route 89A and State Route 179), drive west toward Cottonwood on SR 89A for just under 2 miles and then turn right on Coffeepot Drive. Drive about 0.5 miles and then turn left on Sanborn. Continue to the second street and then turn right on Little Elf. Little Elf ends at Buena Vista so make a short right on Buena Vista and then a quick left into the parking area at GPS coordinates: 34° 52.458' North; 111° 47.793' West {1}. This parking area also serves the Teacup, Thunder Mountain and Sugarloaf trails.

Description: An unmarked, unmaintained trail, this hike takes you to the base of Coffeepot Rock, a well-known Sedona landmark. From the parking lot follow the Sugarloaf Trail until you reach a fork. Bear left {2}. (GPS coordinates 34° 52.793' N; 111 ° 47.673' W). You'll hike on ledges under Coffeepot until the ledges eventually become too narrow and steep to go any farther {3}. Look up and you'll see you are under the spout of Coffeepot {4}.

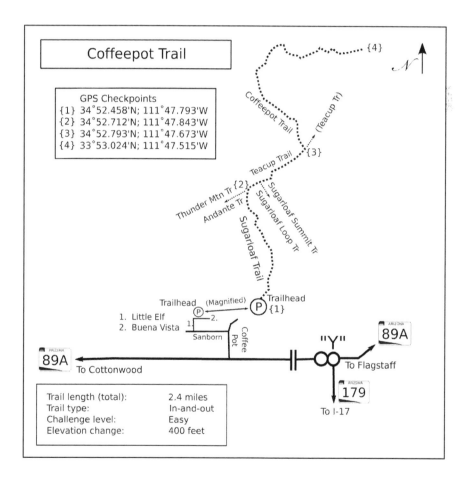

Cookstove to Harding Springs Trail

Summary: A two-vehicle hike up the side of Oak Creek Canyon, through a pine forest and down again

Challenge Level: Hard (and we strongly recommend using a portable GPS unit to hike between the two trails)

Hiking Distance: About 3.2 miles

Trailhead Directions: This is a two-vehicle hike. Park one vehicle at Cave Springs and one at the artesian well at Pine Flats. From the "Y" roundabout (the intersection of State Route 89A and State Route 179), drive north on SR 89A toward Flagstaff for about 11.7 miles (mile marker 385.5) and then turn left into the Cave Springs campground. Park your first vehicle in the parking area on the right {13}. Continue north on SR 89A about 1.2 miles (mile marker 386.8) to the Pine Flats campground. Park the other vehicle on the west side of SR 89A near (but not too near) the well {1}.

Description: Cross SR 89A to the sign for Cookstove and hike up the east side of Oak Creek Canyon. The trail is very steep with many switchbacks and climbs about 1000 feet to a flat mesa. You'll find a trail marker cut into a large pine tree at the top of the trail {2}. Hike south following the edge of Oak Creek Canyon. You'll turn away from Oak Creek Canyon to skirt a side canyon, then make a series of turns {3}{4}{5}. You'll cross several washes and hike along an old road, then rejoin the trail and intersect the Harding Springs Trail {6} {7}{8}{9}{10}. Before starting down the steep Harding Springs Trail (to your other vehicle), continue about 450 feet south along the canyon rim to a nice overlook area {11}. The unmarked, unmaintained trail is difficult to follow at times, and is not a straight line between the top of Cookstove and the Harding Springs Trail. Also, you'll be climbing over many fallen trees. We strongly recommend using a portable GPS unit to hike between the trails across the mesa (see page 7). A shady hike in the summer, with good foliage colors in the fall.

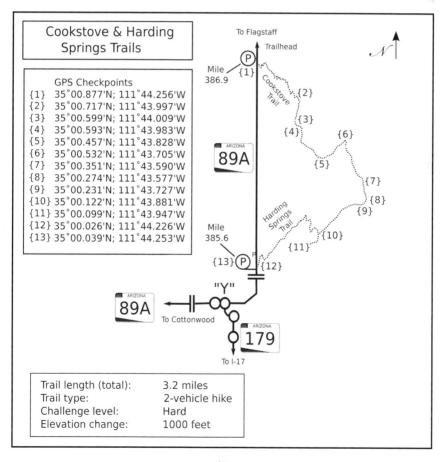

Cookstove & Harding Springs Trails		

GPS Checkpoints
{1} 35°00.877'N; 111°44.256'W
{2} 35°00.717'N; 111°43.997'W
{3} 35°00.599'N; 111°44.009'W
{4} 35°00.593'N; 111°43.983'W
{5} 35°00.457'N; 111°43.828'W
{6} 35°00.532'N; 111°43.705'W
{7} 35°00.351'N; 111°43.590'W
{8} 35°00.274'N; 111°43.577'W
{9} 35°00.231'N; 111°43.727'W
{10} 35°00.122'N; 111°43.881'W
{11} 35°00.099'N; 111°43.947'W
{12} 35°00.026'N; 111°44.226'W
{13} 35°00.039'N; 111°44.253'W

Trail length (total):	3.2 miles
Trail type:	2-vehicle hike
Challenge level:	Hard
Elevation change:	1000 feet

Courthouse Butte Loop Trail

Summary: A pleasant loop hike circling Bell Rock and Courthouse Butte near the Village of Oak Creek

Challenge Level: Moderate

Hiking Distance: About 4 miles round trip

Trailhead Directions: There are two trailhead parking areas for this hike, both along State Route 179. From the "Y" roundabout (the intersection of State Route 89A and State Route 179), drive south on SR 179 for about 5.5 miles. You'll see a "Scenic View" sign on your left, just north of Bell Rock. Turn left here to the first parking area at GPS coordinates: 34° 48.350' North; 111° 46.009' West {1}. There are toilets at the parking area. The trail starts on the southeast side of the parking area on the opposite side from the toilets. You begin hiking 0.2 mile south on a connecting trail that parallels SR 179 on your right. You'll soon intersect the Courthouse Butte Trail.

If you continue on SR 179 another 0.75 mile or so, you'll see another parking area on your left, south of Bell Rock. Turn left into the parking area located at GPS coordinates: 34° 47.501' N; 111° 45.699' W {7}. There are toilets at the parking area. Follow the Bell Rock Pathway Trail north for about 0.5 mile until you intersect the Courthouse Butte Loop Trail.

Description: This trail circling Courthouse Butte and Bell Rock provides good views of these two famous rock formations as well as distant views of Rabbit Ears, the Chapel of the Holy Cross and Cathedral Rock. A good stopping point for a snack break is "Muffin Rock," which some call "UFO Rock" located at GPS coordinates: 34° 48.332' N: 111° 45.012' W {3}.

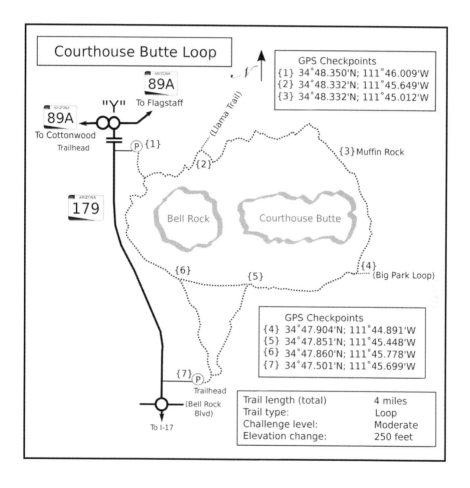

Courthouse Butte Loop

89A

"Y" To Flagstaff

89A
To Cottonwood
Trailhead

(P) {1}

(Llama Trail)

179

GPS Checkpoints
{1} 34°48.350'N; 111°46.009'W
{2} 34°48.332'N; 111°45.649'W
{3} 34°48.332'N; 111°45.012'W

{3} Muffin Rock

{2}

Bell Rock   Courthouse Butte

{6}   {5}   {4}
(Big Park Loop)

GPS Checkpoints
{4} 34°47.904'N; 111°44.891'W
{5} 34°47.851'N; 111°45.448'W
{6} 34°47.860'N; 111°45.778'W
{7} 34°47.501'N; 111°45.699'W

{7} (P)
Trailhead
(Bell Rock
Blvd)

To I-17

Trail length (total)	4 miles
Trail type:	Loop
Challenge level:	Moderate
Elevation change:	250 feet

Cowpies Trail

Summary: An in-and-out stroll over slickrock with nice views all around

Challenge Level: Easy

Hiking Distance: About 1.25 miles each way; 2.5 miles round trip

Trailhead Directions: From the "Y" roundabout (the intersection of State Route 89A and State Route 179), drive south on SR 179 about 0.3 mile to the Schnebly Hill Roundabout and then drive 270 degrees (3/4 of the way) around to Schnebly Hill Road. Proceed 3.5 miles on Schnebly Hill. The trailhead parking is on your right. Use the far entrance to the parking area as the near entrance is very steep and you have a good chance of hitting the bottom of your vehicle. Schnebly Hill is paved for the first mile but the last 2.5 miles can be a very rough unpaved road; a high clearance vehicle is

44

recommended. The parking area is located at GPS coordinates 34° 52.318' North; 111° 42.779' West {1}.

Description: The trailhead is across the road from the parking area. Soon you'll pass by an area dotted with small black rocks, which are pieces of lava. Some believe this to be another powerful vortex area {2}. Sometimes you'll find these rocks placed in the shape of a medicine wheel. Continue along the trail, then make a left turn at GPS coordinates: 34° 52.568' N; 111° 42.914' W {3} to go to the "cowpies" (about at the 0.3 mile mark). If you go straight, you'll be hiking the Mitten Ridge Trail. As you continue to the left, you'll hike up on the "cowpies," which are very large circular red rock formations. There isn't a defined trail so you'll be free to explore the "cowpies."

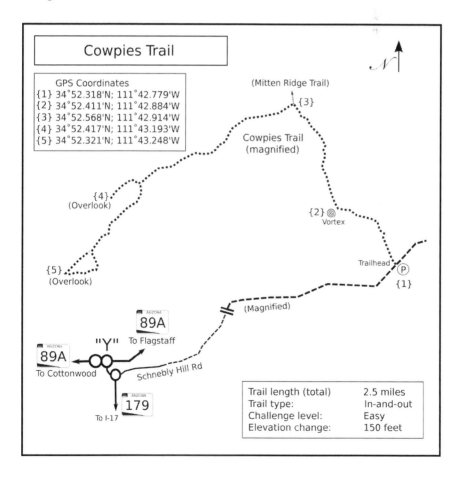

Cowpies Trail

GPS Coordinates
{1} 34°52.318'N; 111°42.779'W
{2} 34°52.411'N; 111°42.884'W
{3} 34°52.568'N; 111°42.914'W
{4} 34°52.417'N; 111°43.193'W
{5} 34°52.321'N; 111°43.248'W

(Mitten Ridge Trail)
{3}
Cowpies Trail
(magnified)
{4}
(Overlook)
{2} Vortex
{5}
(Overlook)
Trailhead
P
{1}
(Magnified)

ARIZONA
89A
"Y" To Flagstaff
ARIZONA
89A
To Cottonwood
Schnebly Hill Rd
ARIZONA
179
To I-17

Trail length (total)	2.5 miles
Trail type:	In-and-out
Challenge level:	Easy
Elevation change:	150 feet

Devil's Bridge Trail

Summary: A moderate in-and-out climb with steep "stairs" up to the largest natural stone arch in the Sedona area

Challenge Level: Moderate

Hiking Distance: About 1 mile each way; 2 miles round trip

Trailhead Directions: From the "Y" roundabout (the intersection of State Route 89A and State Route 179), drive toward Cottonwood on SR 89A for 3 miles. Turn right on Dry Creek Road (where speed limits are strictly enforced). Stay on Dry Creek for about 2 miles and then turn right on Forest Road (FR) 152. Proceed for 1.1 miles to the parking area on your right at GPS coordinates: 34° 54.172' North; 111° 48.833' West {1}. The parking area holds about 8 vehicles so, if it is full, find a spot to pull off the road to park on FR 152. NOTE: FR 152 is an extremely rough road so a high clearance vehicle is recommended.

Description: Devil's Bridge is a large natural stone arch that you can easily walk on. It is reachable with a moderate amount of climbing (up some 400 feet); the view of the arch is well worth the climb. After hiking in about 0.6 mile, there is a very short trail to a scenic overlook on your left {2}{3}. The trail splits about 0.75 mile from the start {4}. Go straight to reach the top of the arch; take the left fork to go beneath the arch. If you take the trail to the top of the arch, you'll be hiking up some steep natural stone steps (with no hand rails) so, if you have a fear of heights, you may want to be extra careful on this hike, or only take the left trail to view the arch from beneath.

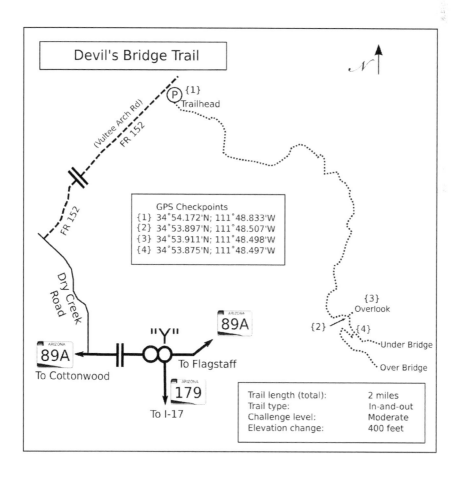

Devil's Bridge Trail

GPS Checkpoints
{1} 34°54.172'N; 111°48.833'W
{2} 34°53.897'N; 111°48.507'W
{3} 34°53.911'N; 111°48.498'W
{4} 34°53.875'N; 111°48.497'W

{3} Overlook
{2} {4}
Under Bridge
Over Bridge

89A
To Cottonwood

"Y"
89A
To Flagstaff

179
To I-17

Trail length (total):	2 miles
Trail type:	In-and-out
Challenge level:	Moderate
Elevation change:	400 feet

Doe Mountain Trail

Summary: Climbs and loops around the top of Doe Mountain, a true, flat-top mesa

Challenge Level: Moderate

Hiking Distance: About 2.6 miles round trip

Trailhead Directions: The parking for Doe Mountain trail is shared with the Bear Mountain trail. From the "Y" roundabout (the intersection of State Route 89A and State Route 179), drive west toward Cottonwood on SR 89A about 3 miles. Turn right on Dry Creek Road (where speed limits are strictly enforced). Stay on Dry Creek to a stop sign (about 3 miles) and then turn left on Boynton Pass Road. Proceed about 1.5 miles to a stop sign. Turn left, continuing on Boynton Pass Road. The trailhead parking is the second one on the left side, about 1.75 miles from the stop sign. The GPS coordinates for the parking lot are: 34° 53.596' North; 111° 51.945' West {1}. The trailhead is at the parking area.

Description: To get to the top of Doe Mountain, you hike up switchbacks. As you approach the rim, you'll pass through a narrow slot in the rocks; pay attention to where you came up (at GPS coordinates: 34° 53.505' N; 111° 51.643' W) {2} by observing your location relative to the parking lot some 400 feet below. It can be hard to find the way back down after hiking around the top of Doe Mountain. The spectacular views are all around.

Although the top of Doe Mountain is crisscrossed with "social" trails, the preferred way is to proceed straight across to the southern side of Doe Mountain and then proceed in a clockwise direction around and then back to the trail down. Another popular way is to go to the left and then skirt the outer edge of the mountain {3}. This way you may be bushwhacking a bit, so be sure to wear hiking boots to protect your ankles from the cactus you'll be stepping over.

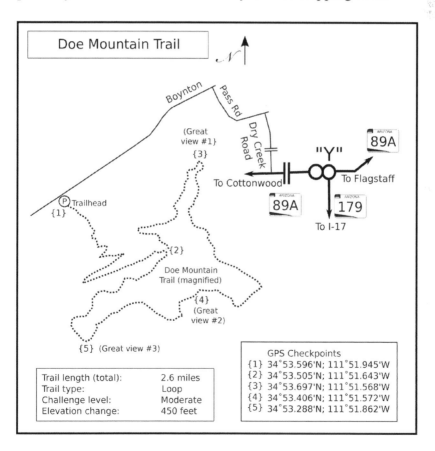

Doe Mountain Trail

Trail length (total):	2.6 miles
Trail type:	Loop
Challenge level:	Moderate
Elevation change:	450 feet

GPS Checkpoints
{1} 34°53.596'N; 111°51.945'W
{2} 34°53.505'N; 111°51.643'W
{3} 34°53.697'N; 111°51.568'W
{4} 34°53.406'N; 111°51.572'W
{5} 34°53.288'N; 111°51.862'W

Dry Creek Trail

Summary: An in-and-out hike through the forest that follows Dry Creek

Challenge Level: Easy to moderate, depending on length of hike

Hiking Distance: About 2.25 miles each way, 4.5 miles round trip

Trailhead Directions: From the "Y" roundabout (the intersection of State Route 89A and State Route 179), drive west toward Cottonwood on SR 89A for 3 miles. Turn right on Dry Creek Road (where speed limits are strictly enforced). Stay on Dry Creek for 2 miles and then turn right on Forest Road (FR) 152. Proceed to the end of FR 152 (about 4.5 miles) to the parking area on the left at GPS coordinates 34° 56.236' North; 111° 47.678' West {1}. NOTE: FR 152 can be an extremely rough road so a high clearance vehicle is recommended. The parking area is the same as used for the Bear Sign and Vultee Arch trails.

Description: This trail follows the path cut by Dry Creek, crossing it about a dozen times. You'll be hiking in a northerly direction and intersect the Bear Sign Trail about 0.8 mile in {2}. As you continue, the canyon cut by Dry Creek gets narrower and you are treated to nice views of towering red rock formations. You can hike another 0.75 mile further up the creek bed if you like.

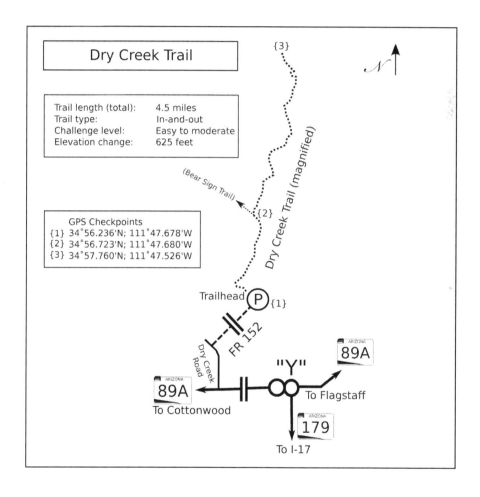

Dry Creek Trail

Trail length (total):	4.5 miles
Trail type:	In-and-out
Challenge level:	Easy to moderate
Elevation change:	625 feet

GPS Checkpoints
{1} 34°56.236'N; 111°47.678'W
{2} 34°56.723'N; 111°47.680'W
{3} 34°57.760'N; 111°47.526'W

Dry Creek Trail (magnified)

(Bear Sign Trail)

Trailhead (P) {1}

FR 152

Dry Creek Road

"Y"

ARIZONA 89A
To Flagstaff

ARIZONA 89A
To Cottonwood

ARIZONA 179
To I-17

Fay Canyon Trail

Summary: A short pleasant in-and-out stroll through a canyon with wonderful red rock formations

Challenge Level: Easy to Moderate

Hiking Distance: About 1.2 miles each way to the rock slide; 2.4 miles round trip

Trailhead Directions: From the "Y" roundabout (the intersection of State Route 89A and State Route 179), drive west toward Cottonwood on SR 89A about 3 miles. Turn right on Dry Creek Road (where speed limits are strictly enforced). Stay on Dry Creek Road (about 3 miles) to the end and a stop sign. Turn left on Boynton Pass Road and then proceed about 1.5 miles to a stop sign. Turn left, continuing on Boynton Pass Road. The trailhead is the first trailhead on the left side, about 0.8 miles from the stop sign. The GPS coordinates for the parking lot are: 34° 54.101' North; 111°

51.450' West {1}. The trailhead is across the road from the parking area.

Description: Fay Canyon is one of our favorite hikes for non-hiker guests because it is short (only about 2.4 miles round trip), and very scenic. The trail looks like it ends at a massive rock slide {4}, but you can climb around on the right side of the slide area and then continue on about another 0.3 mile in a shaded forest if you'd like.

There is a side trail to a natural stone arch about 0.5 mile from the main trailhead (GPS coordinates: 34° 54.507' N; 111° 51.771' W) {2}. You'll have to scramble up this unmarked trail if you want to see the arch, which is located up next to the cliff face {3}. There is also a narrow slot up there where the rocks have separated and you can "disappear" if you can fit into the opening.

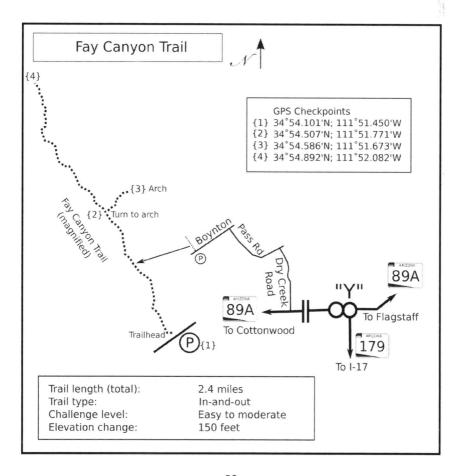

Honanki Indian Ruins

Summary: A loop hike to Sinagua pueblo ruins and rock art tucked under a shallow red rock overhang

Challenge Level: Easy

Hiking Distance: About 0.25 mile each way; 0.5 mile round trip

Trailhead Directions: From the "Y" roundabout (the intersection of State Route 89A and State Route 179), drive west toward Cottonwood on SR 89A about 3 miles. Turn right on Dry Creek Road (where speed limits are strictly enforced) {1}. Stay on Dry Creek to a stop sign (about 3 miles) and then turn left on Boynton Pass Road {2}. Proceed about 1.5 miles to a stop sign. Turn left, continuing on Boynton Pass Road {3}. The first 2 miles is paved, then becomes a gravel road. Drive 4 miles to a stop sign and then turn right on Forest Road (FR) 525 {4}. After about 0.1 mile take the left fork of FR 525 {5} and then continue for another 4.5

miles to the parking area at GPS coordinates: 34° 56.193' North; 111° 56.078' West {6}.

Description: The Pink Jeep Company manages the Honanki site so there are no volunteers or rangers stationed at this site (like at Palatki). You are on your own to wander through the site. There is a metal rail fence to keep unauthorized folks out but you are very close to the structures. There may be people touring the site who are on Jeep tours at the time you are there. The Pink Jeep Company asks that you not interfere with the tours.

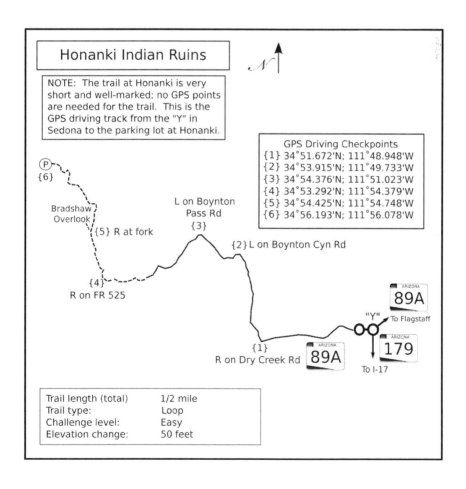

HS Canyon Trail

Summary: A pleasant in-and-out hike through a narrow, forested canyon

Challenge Level: Moderate

Hiking Distance: About 2 miles each way; 4 miles round trip

Trailhead Directions: From the "Y" roundabout (the intersection of State Route 89A and State Route 179), drive west toward Cottonwood on SR 89A for 3 miles. Turn right on Dry Creek Road (where speed limits are strictly enforced). Stay on Dry Creek for 2 miles and then turn right on Forest Road (FR) 152. Proceed on FR 152 for 3.4 miles to the parking area on your left at GPS coordinates: 34° 55.797' North; 111° 48.391' West {1}. NOTE: FR

152 is an extremely rough road so a high clearance vehicle is recommended.

Description: To reach the HS Trail, you begin hiking the Secret Canyon Trail. After about 0.5 mile, you'll see the HS Canyon Trail #50 sign on your left at GPS coordinates 34° 56.299' N; 111° 48.631' W {2}. The trail gently rises about 600 feet providing good red rock views, although the forest obscures some of the views. The name presumably comes from the early settlers finding lots of horse s**t on this trail. A good hike for the hot summer as there is plenty of shade.

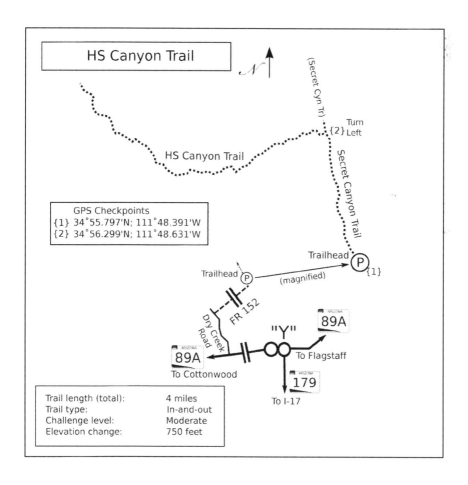

Huckaby Trail

Summary: An in-and-out hike descending from Schnebly Hill Road to the bank of Oak Creek

Challenge Level: Moderate

Hiking Distance: About 2.5 miles each way; 5 miles round trip

Trailhead Directions: From the "Y" roundabout (the intersection of State Route 89A and State Route 179), drive south on SR 179 for about 0.3 mile to the Schnebly Hill roundabout and then drive 270 degrees (3/4 of the way) around to Schnebly Hill Road. Proceed on the paved Schnebly Hill Road for 1 mile and then turn left into the parking area located at GPS coordinates: 34° 52.025' North; 111° 44.946' West {1}. If you start driving on the unpaved Schnebly Hill Road, you've missed the trailhead. Turn around and go back. The trailhead parking is shared with the Munds Wagon trail. The trail begins on the west side of the parking area. There are toilets at the parking area.

Description: The Huckaby trail begins in a westerly direction, then turns north. The trail rises and falls as you approach Oak Creek Canyon. After 1 mile, as you begin to descend to the eastern bank of Oak Creek, there is shade provided by the riparian trees. You have views of "Lucy," "Snoopy," Cathedral Rock and Uptown Sedona. Watch for poison ivy along the trail. Unless the water is low and you want to cross to the other side of Oak Creek by doing some rock-hopping, end the hike where you have an awesome view of Midgley Bridge, just north of Uptown Sedona {2}.

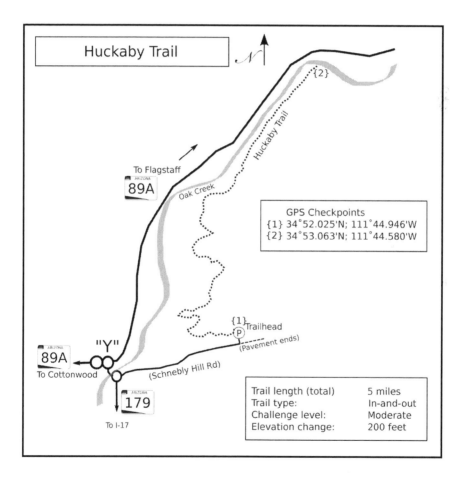

Huckaby Trail

To Flagstaff
89A ARIZONA

Oak Creek

Huckaby Trail

{2}

GPS Checkpoints
{1} 34°52.025'N; 111°44.946'W
{2} 34°53.063'N; 111°44.580'W

{1} Trailhead
(P)
(Pavement ends)

"Y"
89A ARIZONA
To Cottonwood

(Schnebly Hill Rd)

179 ARIZONA
To I-17

Trail length (total)	5 miles
Trail type:	In-and-out
Challenge level:	Moderate
Elevation change:	200 feet

Jim Thompson Trail

Summary: An in-and-out hike to Steamboat Rock overlooking Midgley Bridge.

Challenge Level: Moderate

Hiking Distance: About 2.5 miles each way; 5 miles round trip

Trailhead Directions: From the "Y" roundabout (the intersection of State Route 89A and State Route 179), drive north on SR 89A about 0.25 mile to Jordan Road. Turn left on Jordan Road and then drive to the end. Turn left on Park Ridge Drive and then proceed through the paved cul de sac, continuing on the dirt road for 0.5 mile. The parking is located at GPS coordinates: 34° 53.287' North; 111° 46.098' West {1}. There are toilets at the parking area.

Description: The trail begins on the northeast side of the parking area {2}. You'll begin by hiking north, then quickly turn right and begin hiking south. After hiking 0.4 mile, you'll intersect the end of the Jordan Trail {3}. Soon you'll be hiking in a easterly direction along an old road toward the base of Steamboat Rock. We stopped after about 2.5 miles where you can see the Midgley Bridge and across Oak Creek Canyon {4}. If you continue on for about 0.25 mile, you'll intersect the Wilson Canyon Trail {5}.

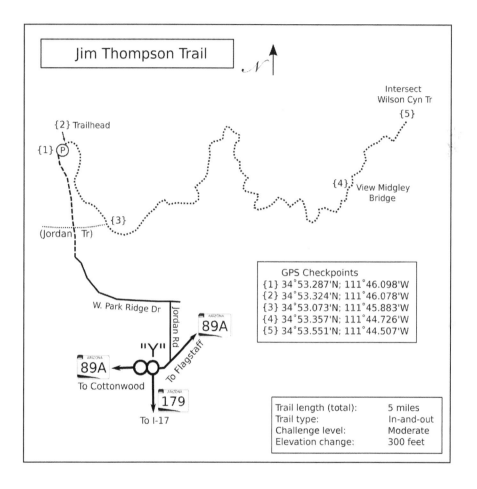

Jordan Trail

Summary: An in-and-out partially shaded hike near town that ends at the Soldier Pass Trail

Challenge Level: Easy to moderate

Hiking Distance: About 1.4 miles each way; 2.8 miles round trip

Trailhead Directions: From the "Y" roundabout (the intersection of State Route 89A and State Route 179), drive north on SR 89A about 0.25 mile to Jordan Road. Turn left on Jordan Road and then drive to the end. Turn left on Park Ridge Drive and then proceed through the paved cul de sac, continuing on the dirt road for 0.5 mile. The parking is located at GPS coordinates: 34° 53.287' North; 111° 46.098' West {1}. There are toilets at the parking area. There are two trailheads for this trail. The trailhead at the parking area is to the right of the toilets. If you walk back down the road 0.4 mile there is another Jordan Trail signpost {2}.

Description: If you begin the hike from the parking area, you'll hike a short distance to the west, then turn south. After 0.4 mile, you'll intersect the second Jordan Trail {3}. If you turn left (east), you'll cross the road and then intersect the Jim Thompson Trail after 0.2 mile. Turn right (west) and then begin hiking the main trail somewhat uphill as you hike along an old road. The views gradually improve as you continue the hike. You'll intersect the Cibola Trail at the 1.1 mile mark {4}. Continue on the Jordan Trail until you intersect the Soldier Pass Trail at Devil's Kitchen, which is a very large sinkhole {5}. If you want to continue a little further, hike north on the Soldier Pass Trail for 0.4 mile to the Seven Sacred Pools {6}. You can retrace your route or hike back on the Cibola Trail to the parking area.

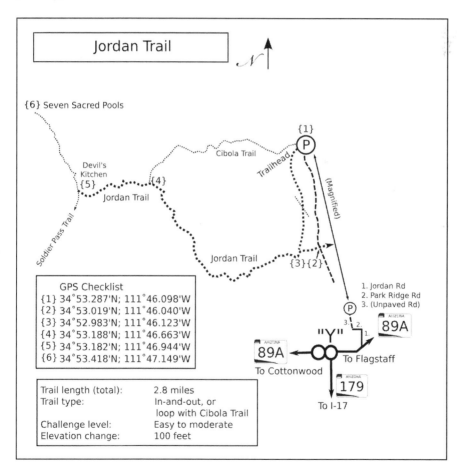

Jordan Trail

{6} Seven Sacred Pools

Cibola Trail

Devil's Kitchen {5} {4}

Jordan Trail

Trailhead {1} P

(Magnified)

Soldier Pass Trail

Jordan Trail

Jordan Trail {3}{2}

GPS Checklist	
{1} 34°53.287'N; 111°46.098'W	
{2} 34°53.019'N; 111°46.040'W	
{3} 34°52.983'N; 111°46.123'W	
{4} 34°53.188'N; 111°46.663'W	
{5} 34°53.182'N; 111°46.944'W	
{6} 34°53.418'N; 111°47.149'W	

1. Jordan Rd
2. Park Ridge Rd
3. (Unpaved Rd)

P

89A

"Y"

89A → To Flagstaff

To Cottonwood

179

To I-17

Trail length (total):	2.8 miles
Trail type:	In-and-out, or loop with Cibola Trail
Challenge level:	Easy to moderate
Elevation change:	100 feet

Kelly Canyon Trail

Summary: A pleasant, shaded in-and-out hike in a ponderosa pine forest with interesting rocks and cliffs

Challenge Level: Easy to Moderate

Hiking Distance: If you hike east Kelly Canyon about 1.3 miles each way; 2.6 miles round trip. If you hike the north Kelly Canyon trail about 2.7 miles each way; 5.5 miles round trip

Trailhead Directions: From the "Y" roundabout (the intersection of State Route 89A and State Route 179), drive north on SR 89A through Uptown Sedona and drive for 17.5 miles. Turn right on a dirt road, (FR 237) at mile marker 390.6, at the north end of a guard rail, {1} 1.5 miles beyond the Oak Creek Vista. Follow the dirt road about 1 mile to a yellow sign with a left arrow. Turn right here {2} on an unmarked faint road near the sign and drive downhill about 500 feet. Park on the flat area at GPS coordinates: 35° 03.501' N; 111° 43.060' W {3}. Hike down the hill on the left (east) and enter Pumphouse Wash {4}. Continue east and hike through the

64

opening in the rocks ahead of you for about 500 feet to the beginning of the trail {5}.

Description: This hike takes you across Pumphouse Wash up Kelly Canyon which is a forested canyon. It is a very peaceful and beautiful hike. There are interesting rock formations as you travel along. At 0.6 mile you'll make a left turn and climb down into the wash {6} to follow the trail. After 1 mile, east Kelly Canyon goes off to the right {7}. If you continue straight you'll follow a well-marked trail along a wash we call north Kelly Canyon. You'll come to a ramp over a downed tree after another 0.3 mile {9}. You'll intersect several trails along the way {10} {11}. After hiking a total of 2.7 miles, you'll intersect FR 237 {12}.

The ambient temperature you encounter on this hike will be cool because of the elevation (about 6400 feet) and the shade provided by the trees. It is a pleasant summer hike, but watch for poison ivy.

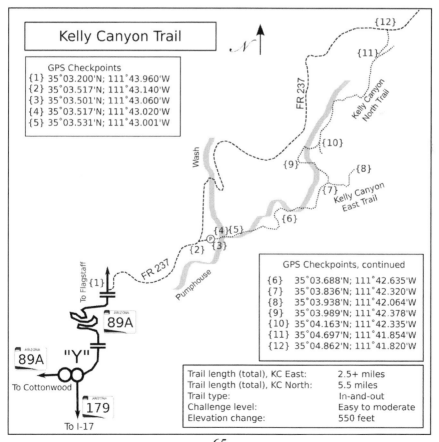

Kelly Canyon Trail

GPS Checkpoints
{1} 35°03.200'N; 111°43.960'W
{2} 35°03.517'N; 111°43.140'W
{3} 35°03.501'N; 111°43.060'W
{4} 35°03.517'N; 111°43.020'W
{5} 35°03.531'N; 111°43.001'W

GPS Checkpoints, continued
{6}   35°03.688'N; 111°42.635'W
{7}   35°03.836'N; 111°42.320'W
{8}   35°03.938'N; 111°42.064'W
{9}   35°03.989'N; 111°42.378'W
{10} 35°04.163'N; 111°42.335'W
{11} 35°04.697'N; 111°41.854'W
{12} 35°04.862'N; 111°41.820'W

Trail length (total), KC East:	2.5+ miles
Trail length (total), KC North:	5.5 miles
Trail type:	In-and-out
Challenge level:	Easy to moderate
Elevation change:	550 feet

Little Horse Trail

Summary: A lovely in-and-out hike to Chicken Point, a large slickrock knoll with majestic views.

Challenge Level: Moderate

Hiking Distance: About 2 miles each way; 4 miles round trip

Trailhead Directions: From the "Y" roundabout (the intersection of State Route 89A and State Route 179), drive south on SR 179 for about 3.5 miles. You'll see a "Scenic View" and a hiking sign on the right side of SR 179. Turn left here and proceed across the median to the parking area at GPS coordinates: 34° 49.433' North; 111° 46.555' West {1}. There are toilets at the parking area.

Description: You'll begin by hiking south on the Bell Rock Pathway for 0.3 mile where it intersects the beginning of the Little Horse Trail at GPS coordinates: 34° 49.301' N; 111 46.308' W {2}. Turn left. When you come to a dry wash, turn left to cross the wash and then follow the trail east and then north toward the Twin Buttes, an impressive red rock formation. You will intersect the Chapel Trail at the 1.4 mile mark (GPS coordinates: 34° 49.705' N; 111° 45.489' W) {3}. Continue on the Little Horse trail for another 0.4 mile and you'll arrive at an expansive area of slickrock. The climb up to Chicken Point isn't hard and is well worth the effort {4}. You'll likely encounter some Pink Jeeps as the "Broken Arrow" tour brings visitors to this beautiful area.

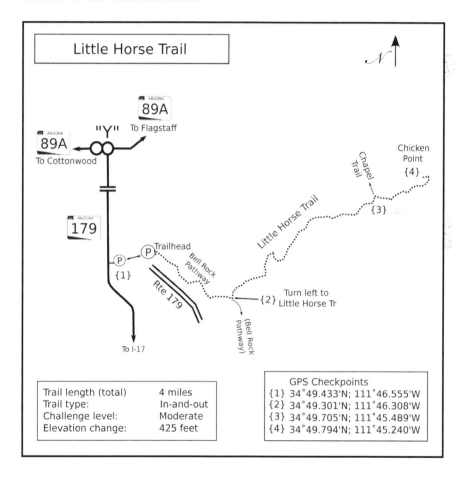

Trail length (total)	4 miles
Trail type:	In-and-out
Challenge level:	Moderate
Elevation change:	425 feet

GPS Checkpoints
{1} 34°49.433'N; 111°46.555'W
{2} 34°49.301'N; 111°46.308'W
{3} 34°49.705'N; 111°45.489'W
{4} 34°49.794'N; 111°45.240'W

Llama Loop Trail

Summary: A loop hike with panoramic views of many of Sedona's famous rock formations

Challenge Level: Easy to Moderate

Hiking Distance: About 4.4 miles round trip

Trailhead Directions: From the "Y" roundabout (the intersection of State Route 89A and State Route 179), drive south on State Route 179 for about 8 miles. The trailhead is the second "scenic view" on the left side of the southbound SR 179 just north of Bell Rock at GPS coordinates: 34° 48.350' North; 111° 46.009' West {1}. There are toilets at the parking area. The trail starts on the southeast side of the parking area. There is another Llama trailhead off of the Little Horse Trail.

Description: Although the Llama Trail goes from Bell Rock to the Little Horse Trail, we prefer to hike it as a loop hike. The 4.4

mile loop beginning on the north side of Bell Rock approaches Lee Mountain and provides outstanding views of Bell Rock, Courthouse Butte, Twin Buttes and Cathedral Rock. There isn't much shade on this hike so it would be a good choice in cooler weather.

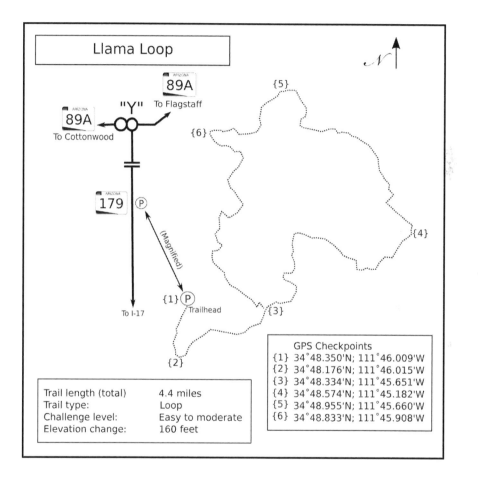

Llama Loop

89A
"Y" To Flagstaff
89A
To Cottonwood
{5}
{6}
{4}
179 Ⓟ
(Magnified)
{1} Ⓟ Trailhead
To I-17
{3}
{2}

Trail length (total)	4.4 miles
Trail type:	Loop
Challenge level:	Easy to moderate
Elevation change:	160 feet

GPS Checkpoints
{1} 34°48.350'N; 111°46.009'W
{2} 34°48.176'N; 111°46.015'W
{3} 34°48.334'N; 111°45.651'W
{4} 34°48.574'N; 111°45.182'W
{5} 34°48.955'N; 111°45.660'W
{6} 34°48.833'N; 111°45.908'W

Long Canyon Trail

Summary: An in-and-out hike through a forested canyon with some red rock views

Challenge Level: Moderate

Hiking Distance: About 3.5 miles each way; 7 miles round trip

Trailhead Directions: From the "Y" roundabout (the intersection of State Route 89A and State Route 179), drive west toward Cottonwood on SR 89A for 3 miles. Turn right on Dry Creek Road (where speed limits are strictly enforced). Stay on Dry Creek

Road to a stop sign (about 3 miles) and then turn right on Long Canyon Road. Proceed 0.6 mile to the parking area on the left at coordinates: 34° 54.396' North; 111° 49.476' West {1}. The trailhead is at the parking area.

Description: This is a nice moderate hike through a canyon with red rock views, although some are obstructed. The first 0.75 mile is not shaded and would be very hot in the summer. But once you are in the forest, the trees provide shade. You intersect the Deadmans Pass Trail about 1 mile in at GPS coordinates: 34° 55.040' N; 111° 49.880' W {2}. We suggest you continue to hike Long Canyon for another 2 miles and then begin the return trip {3}.

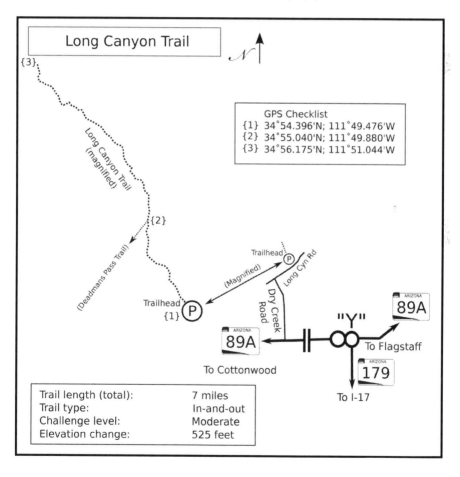

Long Canyon Trail

GPS Checklist
{1} 34°54.396'N; 111°49.476'W
{2} 34°55.040'N; 111°49.880'W
{3} 34°56.175'N; 111°51.044'W

Trail length (total):	7 miles
Trail type:	In-and-out
Challenge level:	Moderate
Elevation change:	525 feet

Lost Canyon Trail

Summary: An in-and-out hike to an overlook of some Indian ruins

Challenge Level: Moderate

Hiking Distance: About 1.25 mile each way; 2.5 miles round trip

Trailhead Directions: From the "Y" roundabout (the intersection of State Route 89A and State Route 179), drive west toward Cottonwood on SR 89A for 3 miles. Turn right on Dry Creek Road (where speed limits are strictly enforced). Stay on Dry Creek for 2 miles and then turn right on Forest Road (FR) 152. Proceed on FR 152 for 2.5 miles to the parking area on your right at GPS coordinates: 34° 55.008' North; 111° 48.525' West {1}. The parking area is for the west end of the Brins Mesa Trail. Hike the Brins Mesa Trail for some 225 feet (about 75 paces) and then turn right to the unmarked Lost Canyon Trail at GPS coordinates: 34° 55.007' N; 111° 48.477' W {2}. NOTE: FR 152 is an extremely rough road so a high clearance vehicle is recommended.

Description: An unmarked, unmaintained trail that climbs from an altitude of about 4625 feet to 4975 feet. The red rock views along the trail are very nice. To see the ruins below, you have to approach the edge of a sheer drop-off; the view is spectacular, but use extreme caution {3}.

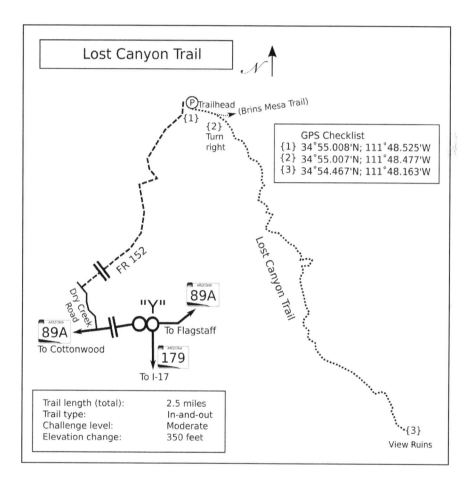

Lost Canyon Trail

N

Trailhead (Brins Mesa Trail)
{1}
{2}
Turn right

GPS Checklist
{1} 34°55.008'N; 111°48.525'W
{2} 34°55.007'N; 111°48.477'W
{3} 34°54.467'N; 111°48.163'W

Lost Canyon Trail

FR 152

Dry Creek Road

"Y"

ARIZONA 89A

ARIZONA 89A
To Cottonwood

To Flagstaff

ARIZONA 179
To I-17

Trail length (total):	2.5 miles
Trail type:	In-and-out
Challenge level:	Moderate
Elevation change:	350 feet

{3}
View Ruins

Marg's Draw Trail

Summary: An in-and-out hike with great red rock views

Challenge Level: Easy to Moderate

Hiking Distance: About 1.3 miles each way from the Sombart Lane Trailhead to Schnebly Hill Road; 2.6 miles round trip

About 2 miles each way from the Morgan Road Trailhead to Schnebly Hill Road; 4 miles round trip

Trailhead Directions: There are actually three trailheads for this hike: at the south end, at the north end and in the middle of the trail. The south trailhead is at the end of Morgan Road, which is located 1.4 miles south of the "Y" roundabout (the intersection of State Route 89A and State Route 179) on SR 179 at GPS coordinates 34° 50.738' North; 111° 45.424' West {1}. The north trailhead is 1 mile up Schnebly Hill Road, (Schnebly Hill Road is located 0.2 mile south of the "Y" on SR 179) at GPS coordinates 34° 52.025' N; 111°

44.946 W' {4}. The middle trailhead is at the end of Sombart Lane, which is located 0.7 mile south of the "Y" (on SR 179 at GPS coordinates 34° 51.427' N; 111° 45.677' W {2}.

Description: The trail essentially goes north and south. The south parking area is shared with Broken Arrow and the north parking area is shared with Huckaby. Hiking from the middle trailhead is steep for the first 0.1 mile, and then is relatively flat {3}. The hike is close to town so there are residences at either end. But in the middle you are in wilderness and have the feeling of being "away from it all."

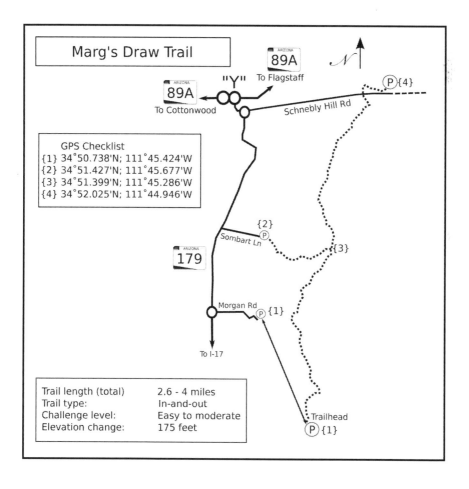

Mescal Mountain Trail

Summary: An in-and-out trail off the Long Canyon Trail with Indian ruins and panoramic views

Challenge Level: Moderate

Hiking Distance: About 1.3 miles each way; 2.6 miles round trip

Trailhead Directions: From the "Y" roundabout (the intersection of State Route 89A and State Route 179), drive west toward Cottonwood on SR 89A about 3 miles. Turn right on Dry Creek Road (where speed limits are strictly enforced). Follow Dry Creek Road to a stop sign (about 3 miles) and then turn right on Long Canyon Road. Proceed 0.6 mile to the parking area on the left at coordinates: 34° 54.396' North; 111° 49.476' West {1}. You'll begin by hiking the Long Canyon Trail for 0.6 mile and then turn left on the unmarked trail at GPS coordinates: 34° 54.747' N; 111° 49.844' W {2}.

Description: This unmarked and unmaintained trail, not found in other guides, is fairly level until you reach the intersection with the side trail leading to "Grandma's Cave" on the right at about 0.3 mile {3}. This short, but steep side trip is well worth the effort to get there. Continuing along the trail to the Mescal Mountain saddle is equally difficult {4}. Near the top you'll climb up to a ledge with a series of shallow caves, where there is evidence of Indian habitation. Continue left along the ledge where there is an area you will need to scramble up to the saddle area. Here there are also early habitation signs and the views are outstanding.

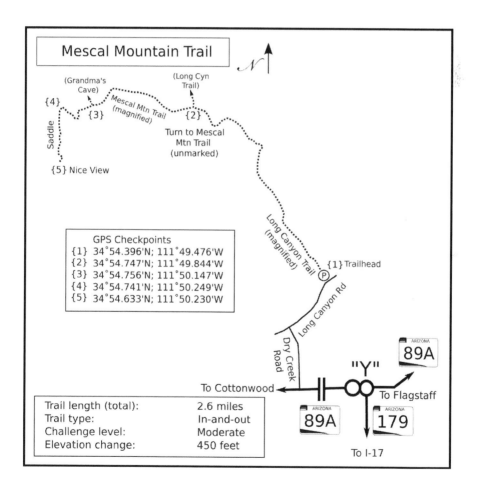

Mescal Mountain Trail

(Grandma's Cave)
(Long Cyn Trail)
Mescal Mtn Trail (magnified)
{4}
{3}
{2}
Saddle
Turn to Mescal Mtn Trail (unmarked)
{5} Nice View

GPS Checkpoints
{1} 34°54.396'N; 111°49.476'W
{2} 34°54.747'N; 111°49.844'W
{3} 34°54.756'N; 111°50.147'W
{4} 34°54.741'N; 111°50.249'W
{5} 34°54.633'N; 111°50.230'W

Long Canyon Trail (magnified)
{1} Trailhead
Long Canyon Rd
Dry Creek Road

ARIZONA 89A

"Y"

To Cottonwood ←
To Flagstaff

ARIZONA 89A
ARIZONA 179

To I-17

Trail length (total):	2.6 miles
Trail type:	In-and-out
Challenge level:	Moderate
Elevation change:	450 feet

Mitten Ridge Trail

Summary: An in-and-out hike along the base of Mitten Ridge

Challenge Level: Moderate (and be sure you have hiking boots with good traction)

Hiking Distance: About 2 miles each way; 4 miles round trip

Trailhead Directions: From the "Y" roundabout (the intersection of State Route 89A and State Route 179), drive south on SR 179 about 0.3 miles to the Schnebly Hill Roundabout and then drive 270 degrees (3/4 of the way) around to Schnebly Hill Road. Proceed 3.5 miles on Schnebly Hill. The trailhead parking is on your right. Use the far entrance to the parking area as the near entrance is very steep and you have a good chance of hitting the bottom of your vehicle. Schnebly Hill is paved for the first mile but the last 2.5 miles can be a very rough unpaved road; a high clearance vehicle is recommended. The parking area is located at GPS coordinates 34°

52.318' North; 111° 42.779' West {1}. The trail begins across the road.

Description: You'll be hiking the Cowpies Trail for the first 0.3 mile. Soon you'll pass by an area dotted with small black rocks, which are pieces of lava. Some believe this to be another powerful vortex area. Sometimes you'll find these rocks placed in the shape of a medicine wheel. Instead of turning left to go to Cowpies {3}, continue straight ahead to the base of Mitten Ridge. The trail turns left at GPS coordinates: 34° 52.637' N; 111° 42.929' W {4}; continue west along the ridge. You'll have to keep your eyes open to follow the trail in some parts. Also, the trail is very narrow with steep drop offs in places. When you arrive at the saddle, which is at the west end of Mitten Ridge, you'll have a nice view of Midgley Bridge and Wilson Mountain to the north {5}.

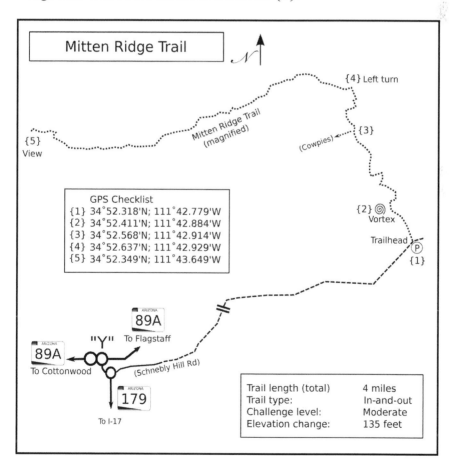

Munds Wagon Trail

Summary: An in-and-out hike following an old road and streambed along Schnebly Hill Road

Challenge Level: Moderate

Hiking Distance: About 2.5 miles each way; 5 miles round trip

Trailhead Directions: From the "Y" roundabout (the intersection of State Route 89A and State Route 179), drive south on SR 179 for about 0.3 mile to the Schnebly Hill Roundabout and then drive 270 degrees (3/4 of the way) around to Schnebly Hill Road. Proceed on Schnebly Hill Road for 1 mile and then turn left in to the parking area located at GPS coordinates: 34° 52.025' North; 111° 44.946' West {1}. If you start driving on the unpaved Schnebly Hill Road you've missed the trailhead. Turn around and go back. The

80

trailhead parking is shared with the Huckaby trail. The trail begins on the east side of the parking area. There are toilets at the parking area.

Description: This hike follows an old wagon trail along Schnebly Hill Road. You cross Schnebly Hill Road once, and then cross back over. If you have a snack with you, there are picnic tables about 1.2 miles along the hike at GPS coordinates: 34° 52.098' N; 111° 44.088' W {2}. We have hiked the trail 2.2 miles each way several times {3}. It is much prettier when there is water flowing from snow runoff, which happens in the spring. The trail becomes harder towards the end (about another 1 mile) as you approach a rock formation known locally as "The Carousel" or "Merry-Go-Round."

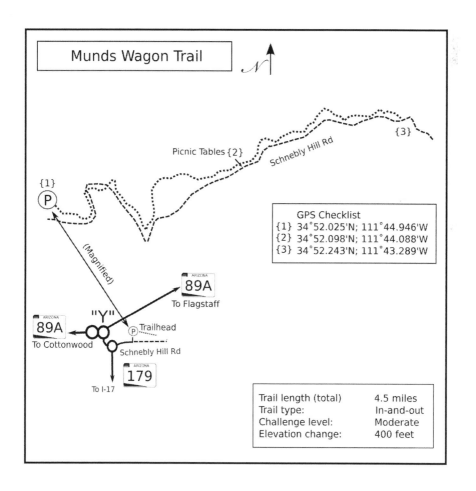

Palatki Indian Ruins

Summary: An in-and-out hike to one of the nicest examples of cliff dwellings and rock art of Native Americans in the Sedona area

Challenge Level: Easy

Hiking Distance: About 0.3 mile each way; 0.6 mile round trip to the ruins. Add another 0.3 mile one way, 0.6 mile round trip to the rock art

Trailhead Directions: From the "Y" roundabout (the intersection of State Route 89A and State Route 179), drive west toward Cottonwood on SR 89A about 3 miles. Turn right on Dry Creek Road (where speed limits are strictly enforced) {1}. Stay on Dry Creek to a stop sign (about 3 miles) and then turn left on Boynton Pass Road {2}. Proceed about 1.5 miles to a stop sign. Turn left, continuing on Boynton Pass Road {3}. The first 2 miles is paved, then becomes a gravel road. Drive 4 miles to a stop sign and then turn right on Forest Road (FR) 525 {4}. After about 0.1 mile take the right fork, {5} which is FR 795, and then continue for another 1.75 miles to the parking area at GPS coordinates: 34° 54.963' North; 111° 54.141' West {6}.

Description: Because parking is limited at this Heritage Site, you must make a reservation by calling (928) 282-3854; however, there is no cost beyond the cost of a Red Rock Pass (or equivalent). When making a reservation, the ranger will ask your last name, how many in your party and which time slot you want (9:30 am, 11:30 am, or 1:30 pm). After you park, walk to the Visitor Center and check in. Then continue down the path and either go right to the ruins, or left to the rock art. There are rangers and volunteers on duty to give the site's history and answer questions.

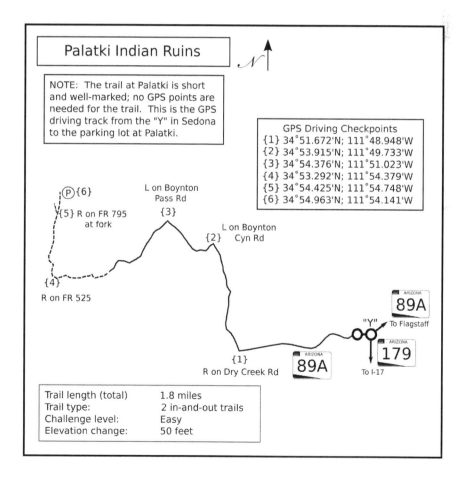

Pyramid Trail

Summary: An in-and-out hike up the back side of the "great pyramid," which is visible from the end of the Tabletop Trail off the west side of the Airport Loop Trail.

Challenge Level: Moderate but the trail up to the summit of the pyramid is very steep

Hiking Distance: About 1.5 miles each way; 3 miles round trip

Trailhead Directions: From the "Y" roundabout (the intersection of State Route 89A and State Route 179), drive west on SR 89A for about 4.25 miles and then turn left on the Upper Red Rock Loop Road. Follow the Upper Loop Road for 1.4 miles. There are two places to park. The first place is a large parking area on the left side of the road at GPS coordinates: 34° 50.202' North; 111° 49.302' West {1}. Then walk down the road for 0.2 mile to GPS coordinates: 34° 50.100' N; 111° 49.218' W and then turn right to the trail {2}.

To park at the second area along the road, drive 0.3 mile past the first area and park on the right side of the Upper Loop Road at GPS coordinates: 34° 50.096' N; 111° 49.119' W {3}. There is another access trail here.

Description: An unmarked and unmaintained trail you won't find in other guides, it begins off the Upper Red Rock Loop Road at GPS coordinates: 34° 50.100' N; 111 49.218' W {2}. You'll pass through an opening in a fence after 0.1 mile {4}. Hike westward to a saddle and then turn left. The trail is easy to follow but has loose rock and is steep in places, particularly the section of the trail leading to the pyramid summit {5}{6}. From the top, the view of Cathedral Rock is remarkable. And for the best photos, hike in the afternoon. Backtrack down the pyramid to the saddle junction, but go straight to follow the trail around to a point with wonderful views of Oak Creek, Mingus Mountain and Red Rock State Park {6}.

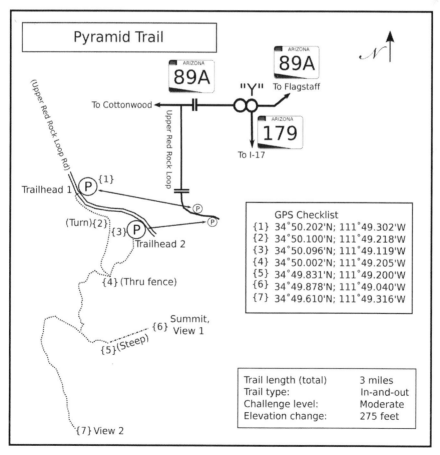

Pyramid Trail

GPS Checklist
{1} 34°50.202'N; 111°49.302'W
{2} 34°50.100'N; 111°49.218'W
{3} 34°50.096'N; 111°49.119'W
{4} 34°50.002'N; 111°49.205'W
{5} 34°49.831'N; 111°49.200'W
{6} 34°49.878'N; 111°49.040'W
{7} 34°49.610'N; 111°49.316'W

Trail length (total)	3 miles
Trail type:	In-and-out
Challenge level:	Moderate
Elevation change:	275 feet

Schuerman Mountain Trail

Summary: An in-and-out hike up the side of a mountain with wonderful panoramic views of Cathedral Rock and other notable landmarks

Challenge Level: Moderate

Hiking Distance: About 1 mile to the top, then another 0.25 miles to the southern overlook; 2.5 miles round trip

Trailhead Directions: From the "Y" roundabout (the intersection of State Route 89A and State Route 179), drive west toward Cottonwood on SR 89A for 4.25 miles. Turn left on the Upper Red Rock Loop Road. Sedona High School is on your right. Turn right at the third driveway (it's behind the school) and then look immediately for the sign to the trailhead parking area on the left at GPS coordinates: 34° 50.762' North; 111° 49.716' West {1}.

Description: Schuerman Mountain provides great views of Cathedral Rock and other red rock views. If you hike in April, you may encounter wildflowers blooming. When you get to the top of Schuerman Mountain {2}, take the trail to the left (south) for a good view of Cathedral Rock {3}. You can also take the trail to the right to the top to look west toward the Verde Valley and Mingus Mountain.

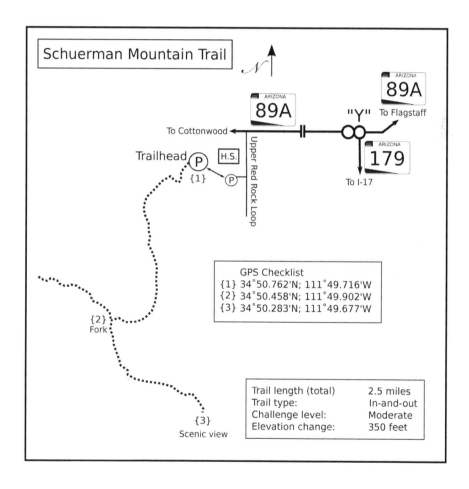

87

Secret Canyon Trail

Summary: An in-and-out hike up a beautiful red rock canyon

Challenge Level: Moderate

Hiking Distance: About 2.4 miles each way; 4.8 miles round trip

Trailhead Directions: From the "Y" roundabout (the intersection of State Route 89A and State Route 179), drive west toward Cottonwood on SR 89A for 3 miles. Turn right on Dry Creek Road (where speed limits are strictly enforced). Stay on Dry Creek for 2 miles and then turn right on Forest Road (FR) 152. Proceed on FR 152 for 3.4 miles to the parking area on your left at GPS coordinates: 34° 55.797' North; 111° 48.391' West {1}. NOTE: FR 152 is an extremely rough road so a high clearance vehicle is recommended.

Description: This hike goes up a very picturesque canyon. You'll encounter the HS Trail about 0.7 mile into the hike {2} and the

David Miller Trail about 2 miles into the hike {3}. At about 2.25 miles you'll be in a pine forest. We usually stop after hiking 2.4 miles, but the trail continues on another 2 miles, becoming steeper and rockier.

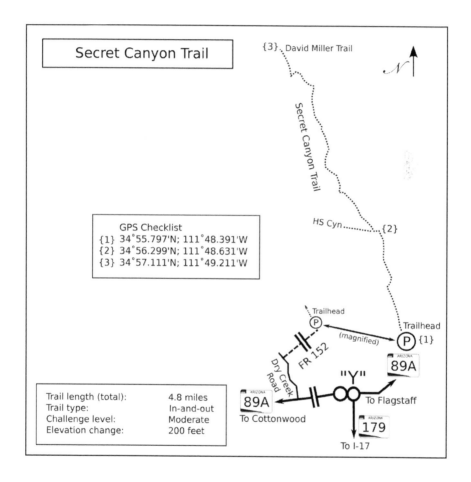

Secret Canyon Trail

{3} David Miller Trail

Secret Canyon Trail

GPS Checklist
{1} 34°55.797'N; 111°48.391'W
{2} 34°56.299'N; 111°48.631'W
{3} 34°57.111'N; 111°49.211'W

HS Cyn .... {2}

Trailhead

(magnified)

Trailhead
{1}

FR 152

Dry Creek Road

"Y"

ARIZONA
89A

Trail length (total):	4.8 miles
Trail type:	In-and-out
Challenge level:	Moderate
Elevation change:	200 feet

ARIZONA
89A

To Cottonwood

To Flagstaff

ARIZONA
179

To I-17

Soldier Pass Trail

Summary: An in-and-out hike with stops at the Devil's Kitchen and the Seven Sacred Pools with views of some impressive red rock arches

Challenge Level: Moderate

Hiking Distance: About 1.5 miles each way, 3 miles round trip; about 2.5 miles one way to the Brins Mesa Trail; 5 miles round trip.

Trailhead Directions: From the "Y" roundabout (the intersection of State Route 89A and State Route 179), drive west toward Cottonwood on SR 89A for 1.25 miles and then turn right on Soldier Pass Road. Proceed on Soldier Pass for 1.5 miles. Turn right on Rim Shadows. Go approximately 0.25 mile and then turn left into the parking area at GPS coordinates: 34° 53.057' North; 111° 47.028' West {1}. The gate to the parking area is open from 8:00 am to 6:00 pm. If you get back to your car after 6:00 pm, you won't be able to drive out of the parking area.

Description: Shortly after beginning the Soldier Pass Trail, you arrive at the Devil's Kitchen (about 0.2 mile) {2}. This is the largest sinkhole in the Sedona area. After another 0.4 mile, you'll come to the Seven Sacred Pools, which are small depressions in the red rock that hold water even in dry periods {3}. These two areas are very popular, but you won't encounter as many other hikers on the rest of the trail. About 1.3 miles from the trailhead, look to the right (at GPS coordinates: 34° 53.865' N; 111° 47.269' W) for a view of the Soldier Pass Arches {4}. As you continue, the trail becomes rockier and steeper as it approaches the end at Brins Mesa; about 2.5 miles from the trailhead {5}.

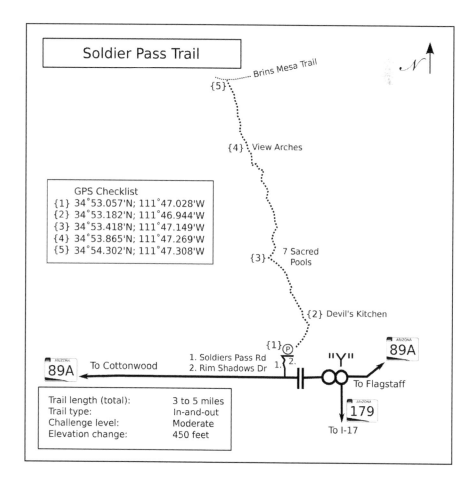

Soldier Pass Trail

Brins Mesa Trail

{5}

{4} View Arches

GPS Checklist
{1} 34°53.057'N; 111°47.028'W
{2} 34°53.182'N; 111°46.944'W
{3} 34°53.418'N; 111°47.149'W
{4} 34°53.865'N; 111°47.269'W
{5} 34°54.302'N; 111°47.308'W

{3} 7 Sacred Pools

{2} Devil's Kitchen

{1}

ARIZONA 89A

To Cottonwood

1. Soldiers Pass Rd
2. Rim Shadows Dr

"Y"

ARIZONA 89A

To Flagstaff

Trail length (total):	3 to 5 miles
Trail type:	In-and-out
Challenge level:	Moderate
Elevation change:	450 feet

ARIZONA 179

To I-17

Sterling Pass to Vultee Arch Trail

Summary: An in-and-out or a two vehicle "pass-the-key" hike up the west side of Oak Creek Canyon then down to Secret Mountain Wilderness

Challenge Level: Hard

Hiking Distance: About 3 miles from the Sterling Pass parking area to the Vultee Arch parking area: about 2.4 miles each way; 4.8 miles round trip as an in-and-out hike from Sterling Pass trailhead to Vultee Arch

Trailhead Directions: From the "Y" roundabout (the intersection of State Route 89A and State Route 179), drive north on SR 89A toward Flagstaff for 6.25 miles. You'll need to find a wide spot in the road to park on the west side. The trail starts at GPS coordinates: 34° 56.185' North; 111° 44.829' West on the west side of SR 89A {1}. We prefer to do this hike as a "pass-the-key" two-vehicle hike (i.e. two groups hiking toward each other from the two separate trailheads and exchanging their vehicle keys) with one vehicle parked at the Sterling Pass trailhead and the other parked at the Vultee Arch trailhead at the end of FR 152 {4} (see the Vultee Arch information for trailhead directions).

Description: The parking along SR 89A isn't the best, as there is no official parking area. You'll need to find a wide shoulder near the trailhead. The trail is steep. You'll climb about 1000 feet and then enter a pine forest. After you reach the saddle, the trail starts down. About 1.5 miles in, you'll come to the sign for Vultee Arch {3}. Hike 0.25 mile down the Vultee Arch Trail to see Vultee Arch, an impressive sight (see Vultee Arch hike description), If you only have one vehicle, retrace your steps back to your vehicle parked along SR 89A.

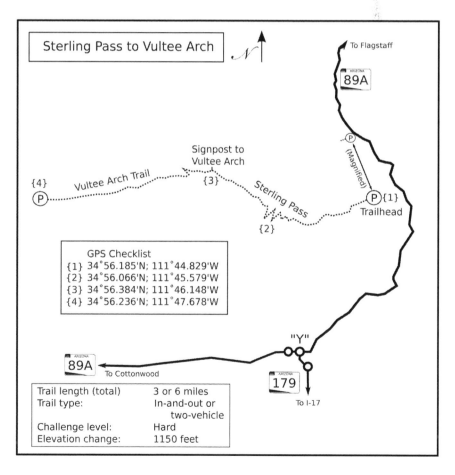

Sterling Pass to Vultee Arch

To Flagstaff

89A

Signpost to
Vultee Arch

{4}   Vultee Arch Trail   {3}   Sterling Pass

(P)   (P){1}
Trailhead

{2}

GPS Checklist
{1} 34°56.185'N; 111°44.829'W
{2} 34°56.066'N; 111°45.579'W
{3} 34°56.384'N; 111°46.148'W
{4} 34°56.236'N; 111°47.678'W

"Y"

89A ←
To Cottonwood

179

To I-17

Trail length (total)	3 or 6 miles
Trail type:	In-and-out or two-vehicle
Challenge level:	Hard
Elevation change:	1150 feet

Sugarloaf Trail

Summary: An in-and-out hike with nice views of Capital Butte, Coffeepot and Sedona

Challenge Level: Moderate

Hiking Distance: About 1.6 miles each way; 3.3 miles round trip

Trailhead Directions: From the "Y" roundabout (the intersection of State Route 89A and State Route 179) drive west toward Cottonwood on SR 89A for just under 2 miles and then turn right on Coffeepot Drive. Drive about 0.5 mile and then turn left on Sanborn. Continue to the second street and then turn right on Little Elf. Little Elf ends at Buena Vista so make a short right on Buena Vista and then a quick left into the parking area at GPS coordinates: 34 ° 52.459' North; 111° 47.780' West {1}. This is the same parking area as the Coffeepot Trail.

Description: From the parking area go north along the base of Sugarloaf, then at GPS coordinates: 34° 52.712' N; 111° 47.843' W turn east {2}. At GPS coordinates: 34° 52.735' N; 111° 47.689' W turn right (south) {3} to hike to the top {4}. From the top you'll have panoramic views all around.

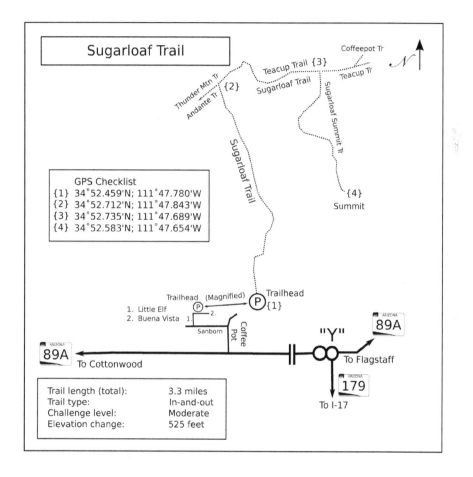

Templeton Trail

Summary: A sunny in-and-out hike around the base of Cathedral Rock

Challenge Level: Moderate

Hiking Distance: About 2 miles each way; 4 miles round trip

Trailhead Directions: We used the Cathedral Rock Trailhead for this hike. From the "Y" roundabout (the intersection State Route 89A and State Route 179), drive south on SR 179 for 3.2 miles to the Back' O Beyond roundabout. Go west on the Back 'O Beyond Road for about 0.75 mile. The parking area is on your left at GPS coordinates 34° 49.523' North; 111° 47.303' West {1}. The trailhead is at the west end of the parking area.

Description: The Templeton Trail actually extends from SR 179 to the Baldwin Trail near Oak Creek, but we prefer to hike from Cathedral Rock to SR 179 and then back. The Cathedral Rock Trail intersects the middle of the Templeton Trail under Cathedral Rock {2}. We prefer to hike east (left) until we connect to the H. T. Trail. We then follow the H. T. Trail until we find a nice stopping point just short of Highway 179 {4}. The trail has excellent views of Cathedral Rock and many other red rock formations.

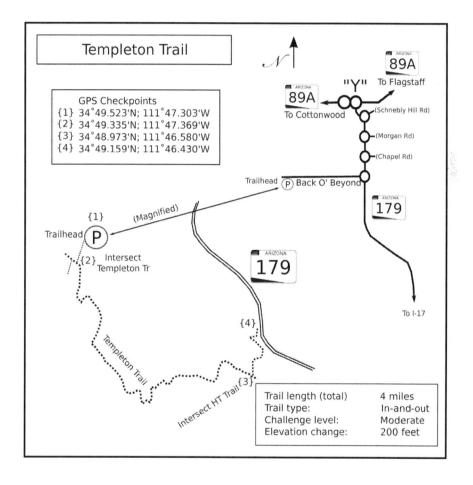

Templeton Trail

GPS Checkpoints
{1} 34°49.523'N; 111°47.303'W
{2} 34°49.335'N; 111°47.369'W
{3} 34°48.973'N; 111°46.580'W
{4} 34°49.159'N; 111°46.430'W

Trail length (total)		4 miles
Trail type:		In-and-out
Challenge level:		Moderate
Elevation change:		200 feet

Turkey Creek/House Mountain Trail

Summary: A sunny, in-and-out hike through fields, then up steep switchbacks to the summit of House Mountain

Challenge Level: Hard

Hiking Distance: About 3.5 miles each way; 7 miles round trip

Trailhead Directions: From the "Y" roundabout (the intersection of State Route 89A and State Route 179), drive south on SR 179 just over 7 miles to the roundabout, which connects SR 179, Jack's Canyon and Verde Valley School Road. Turn right on Verde Valley School Road and then drive for 4 miles to GPS coordinates 34° 48.736' North; 111° 48.540' West {1}. Turn left here on Forest Road 9216B and then drive for about 0.6 mile to the parking area at GPS coordinates 34° 48.571' N; 111° 49.070' W {2}.

Description: From the parking area, hike south on an old road for about 0.3 mile until you reach a fork in the trail at GPS coordinates:

34° 48.340' N; 111° 49.067' W {3}. Take the fork to the right to follow the Turkey Creek Trail; the left trail leads to the Twin Pillars. Follow the Turkey Creek Trail for another 1.3 miles and you reach the first of several "tanks" (a man-made depression in the ground that occasionally fills with water) as you approach House Mountain. Along the way, you cross Turkey Creek. Climb up House Mountain for some wonderful views of the red rocks {6}. It's a long steep climb up to the top of House Mountain, but worth the effort.

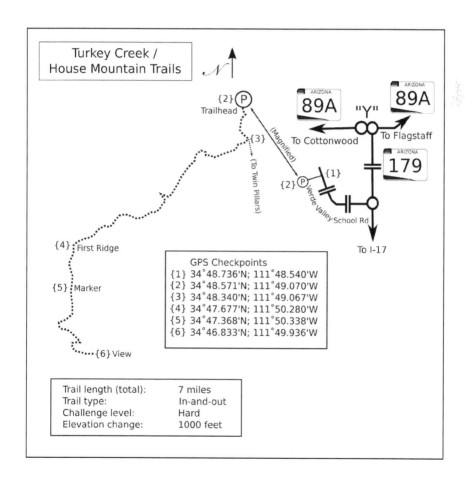

V-Bar-V Petroglyph Site

Summary: A short in-and-out hike to the largest example of petroglyphs in the area

Challenge Level: Easy

Hiking Distance: About 0.5 miles each way; 1 mile round trip

Trailhead Directions: From the "Y" roundabout (the intersection of State Route 89A and State Route 179), drive south on SR 179 for 14.75 miles to the intersection of Interstate 17. Drive under I-17 and then continue for another 2.75 miles. Turn right {1} into the parking area located at GPS coordinates: 34° 39.986' North; 111° 42.942' West {2}.

Description: Located south of I-17 off of Forest Road 618, the V-Bar-V petroglyph site is a unique experience. It is an easy 0.5 mile hike from the Visitor Center {3} to the rock art site {4} (but the path gets very muddy in wet weather). The views of prehistoric rock art are excellent. Note: the site is normally open Friday through Monday, 9:30 am to 3:30 pm, but you should check with the Sedona Chamber of Commerce Visitor Center or at the Forest Service Ranger Station for days of operation. You do not need a reservation; however, a Red Rock Pass is required to park.

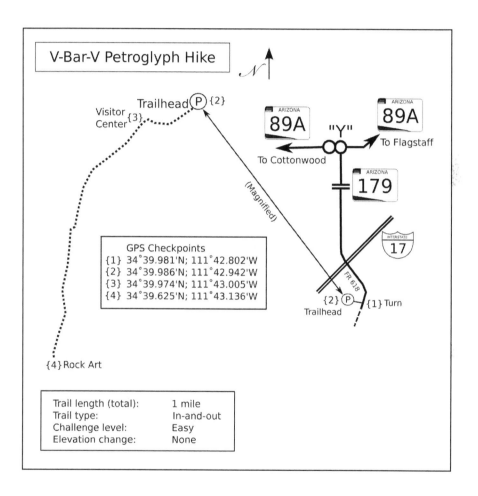

Vultee Arch Trail

Summary: A shady in-and-out hike to a natural red rock arch

Challenge Level: Easy to moderate

Hiking Distance: About 1.6 miles one way to view the arch, add another 0.3 mile to climb up on the arch; 3.2 miles round trip

Trailhead Directions: From the "Y" roundabout (the intersection of State Route 89A and State Route 179), drive west toward Cottonwood on SR 89A for 3 miles. Turn right on Dry Creek Road (where speed limits are strictly enforced). Stay on Dry Creek for 2 miles and then turn right on Forest Road (FR) 152. Proceed to the end of FR 152 (about 4.5 miles) to the parking area on the left at GPS coordinates 34° 56.236' North; 111° 47.678' West {1}. NOTE: FR 152 can be an extremely rough road so a high clearance vehicle is recommended. The parking area is the same as used for the Bear Sign and Dry Creek trails.

Description: The hike to the arch viewpoint is a relatively easy hike, but it is a scramble (thus the moderate hike rating) to get to the arch so be careful if you attempt this. The arch is located at GPS coordinates: 34° 56.500' N; 111° 46.123' W {3}. Vultee Arch is named after Gerald and Sylvia Vultee who crashed their plane and died nearby in 1938. There is a plaque dedicated to them near the arch.

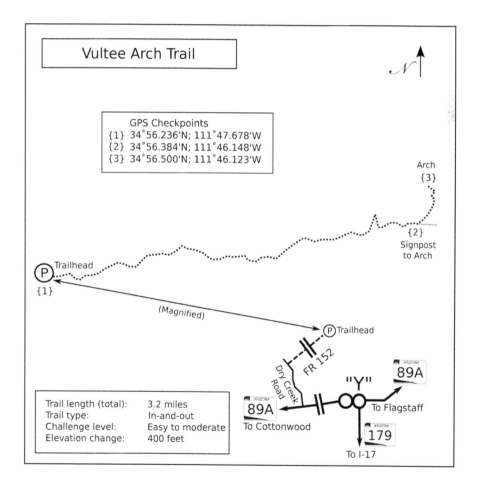

Weir Trail

Summary: A sunny in-and-out trail that follows the path of Wet Beaver Creek

Challenge Level: Moderate

Hiking Distance: About 3 miles each way to the weir (a low dam); 6 miles round trip

Trailhead Directions: From the "Y" roundabout (the intersection of State Route 89A and State Route 179), drive south on SR 179 for 14.75 miles until it intersects Interstate 17. Continue under I-17 and then proceed straight on FR 618 for 2 miles and then turn left at the sign for the Beaver Creek Ranger Station. Follow the dirt road a short distance to the parking area at GPS coordinates: 34° 40.457' North; 111° 42.795' West {1}. There are toilets at the trailhead.

Description: To reach the Weir Trail, follow the Bell Trail along Wet Beaver Creek for a few miles. This can be a very hot hike in the summer as there is no shade for most of the hike. You will come across several trails as you hike along. The first one is the White Mesa Trail at about 1.75 miles {2}. The next trail you come across is the Apache Maid Trail at 2.25 miles {3}. You'll intersect the short Weir Trail in another 0.2 mile, which goes down to the creek. While the rock-strewn Bell Trail goes on, a good stopping place is at the weir in the shade {5}.

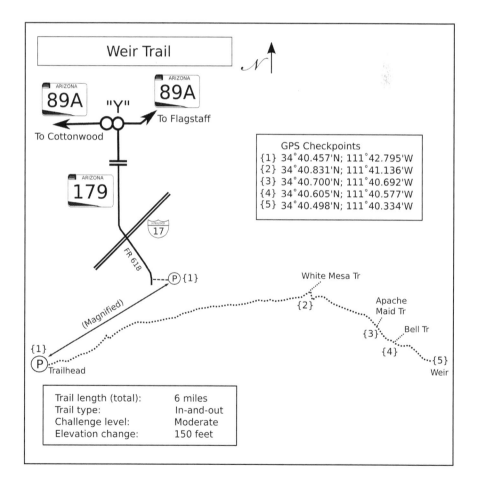

West Fork Trail

Summary: A shady in-and-out hike along a flowing creek

Challenge Level: Moderate

Hiking Distance: About 3.3 miles each way; 6.6 miles round trip

Trailhead Directions: From the "Y" roundabout (the intersection of State Route 89A and State Route 179), drive north on SR 89A toward Flagstaff for 10.5 miles. Turn left in to the parking area located at GPS coordinates: 34° 59.446' North; 111° 44.570' West {1}. The trail starts on the far side of the parking area, furthest away from the entrance. There are toilets at the parking area.

Description: Perhaps the most beautiful trail in the Sedona area, the West Fork hike is one of our favorites. West Fork is a special fee area (see Required Parking Pass, page 6). You'll be crossing the water about a dozen times as you hike the trail. You have to step from stone to stone to cross, so the hike isn't recommended in high water times (you'll get your feet wet!!). After 0.3 mile you'll come to the remains of Mayhew's Lodge, built in the 1800's. It was remodeled in 1895 and then burned down in 1980 {2}. At the 0.4 mile mark you'll come to the first of 13 creek crossings {3}. As you continue along, look to the sides for some amazing red rock bluffs. There is a nice spot to stop after 1 mile {4}. At 2.2 miles you'll come to a huge overhang where the water has eroded the rock {5}. Continue another 0.2 mile and watch for a short side trail to a cave on your left {6}. At 3.3 miles you'll effectively come to the end of the trail because you'll have to wade through the water to continue {7}.

West Fork has two wonderful seasons, spring and fall. The most beautiful is fall, when the deciduous trees display glorious colors. The third week in October seems to be when the colors are at their peak.

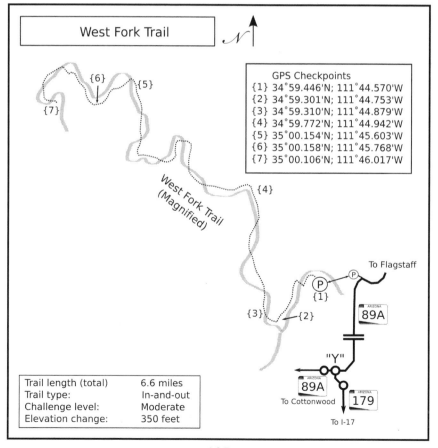

West Fork Trail

GPS Checkpoints
{1} 34°59.446'N; 111°44.570'W
{2} 34°59.301'N; 111°44.753'W
{3} 34°59.310'N; 111°44.879'W
{4} 34°59.772'N; 111°44.942'W
{5} 35°00.154'N; 111°45.603'W
{6} 35°00.158'N; 111°45.768'W
{7} 35°00.106'N; 111°46.017'W

West Fork Trail (Magnified)

To Flagstaff

ARIZONA 89A

"Y"

ARIZONA 89A
To Cottonwood

ARIZONA 179
To I-17

Trail length (total)	6.6 miles
Trail type:	In-and-out
Challenge level:	Moderate
Elevation change:	350 feet

Wilson Canyon Trail

Summary: A pleasant in-and-out hike in a shaded canyon with red rock views

Challenge Level: Moderate

Hiking Distance: About 1.5 miles each way; 3 miles round trip

Trailhead Directions: From the "Y" roundabout (the intersection of State Route 89A and State Route 179), drive north toward Flagstaff on SR 89A to the Midgley Bridge. The trailhead parking is on your left just as you cross the bridge at GPS coordinates: 34° 53.143' North; 111° 44.501' West {1}. The parking lot can fill up quickly on the weekends.

Description: The trailhead is away from SR 89A at the far end of the parking area. At first, the trail is wide but narrows further on. At about 0.5 mile, you'll intersect the end of the Jim Thompson Trail {3}. The Wilson Canyon trail crosses the bottom of the canyon about a dozen times as it winds in about 1.6 miles. At first, the trees obstruct the views. But as you approach the end of the trail, you begin hiking uphill and the views are much better {4}.

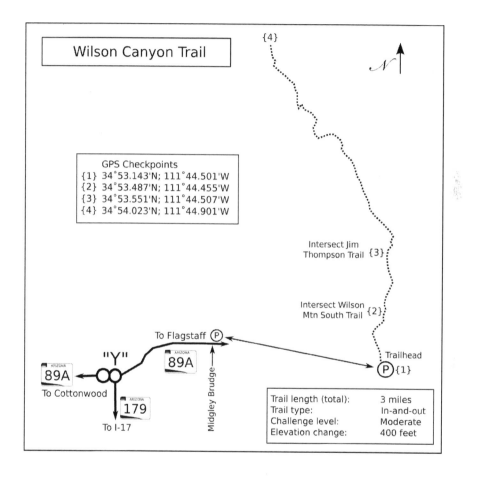

Wilson Mountain South Trail

Summary: A sunny in-and-out hike to the top of Wilson Mountain, the highest mountain in the Sedona area.

Challenge Level: Hard

Hiking Distance: About 5 miles each way to the top; 10 miles round trip

Trailhead Directions: From the "Y" roundabout (the intersection of State Route 89A and State Route 179), drive north toward Flagstaff on SR 89A to the Midgley Bridge. The trailhead parking is on your left just as you cross the bridge at GPS coordinates: 34° 53.143' North; 111° 44.501' West {1}. The parking lot can fill up quickly on the weekends

Description: From the Midgley Bridge parking area you'll hike up switchbacks for 2.4 miles with a 1,600 foot elevation change to the "first bench," a long plateau running the length of the east side of the mountain {3}. From there, you go another mile and 800 feet higher to the tool shed where fire tools are stored. From there, you turn left/south to a high point (7000+ feet, the highest mountain in Sedona). At the top, you can see the San Francisco Peaks to the north in Flagstaff. Go another 0.25 mile to the edge for fantastic views overlooking Sedona {4}. The trail is snowy in the winter!!! Difficult but worth it!

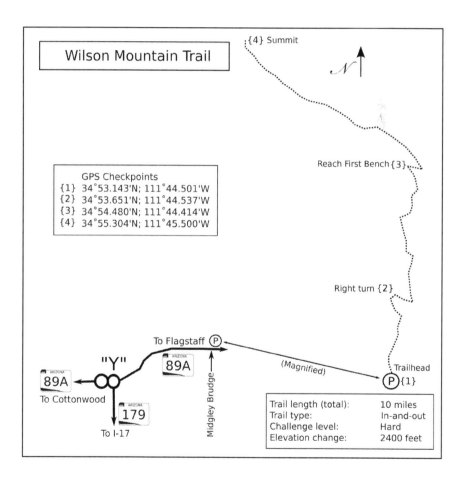

Wilson Mountain Trail

{4} Summit

Reach First Bench {3}

GPS Checkpoints
{1} 34°53.143'N; 111°44.501'W
{2} 34°53.651'N; 111°44.537'W
{3} 34°54.480'N; 111°44.414'W
{4} 34°55.304'N; 111°45.500'W

Right turn {2}

To Flagstaff (P)

"Y"

89A   ARIZONA 89A

To Cottonwood   ARIZONA 179

To I-17

Midgley Brudge

(Magnified)

Trailhead
(P){1}

Trail length (total):	10 miles
Trail type:	In-and-out
Challenge level:	Hard
Elevation change:	2400 feet

Woods Canyon Trail

Summary: A pleasant in-and-out hike along Dry Beaver Creek

Challenge Level: Moderate

Hiking Distance: About 2.5 miles each way; 5 miles round trip

Trailhead Directions: From the "Y" roundabout (the intersection of State Route 89A and State Route 179), drive south on SR 179 for 8.75 miles and then turn in to the Ranger Station at GPS coordinates 34° 45.371' North; 111° 45.890' West {1}. Follow the drive and then turn right at the first road rather than following the road to the left to the Visitor Center. The trailhead is at the far south end of the parking area {2}.

Description: Just after you begin the trail, you will cross a small ditch, which always has water in it. The trail proceeds up a canyon and follows the path of Dry Beaver Creek. You'll intersect the Hot Loop Trail about 2 miles in {4}. Continue straight on Woods Canyon until you come to an area with large river rocks (at GPS coordinates: 34° 45.628' N; 111° 43.642' W), which are left when Dry Beaver Creek flows heavily {5} {6}. We usually stop there, but the trail continues on, becoming more difficult the further you go. Wildflowers are in abundance in April most years.

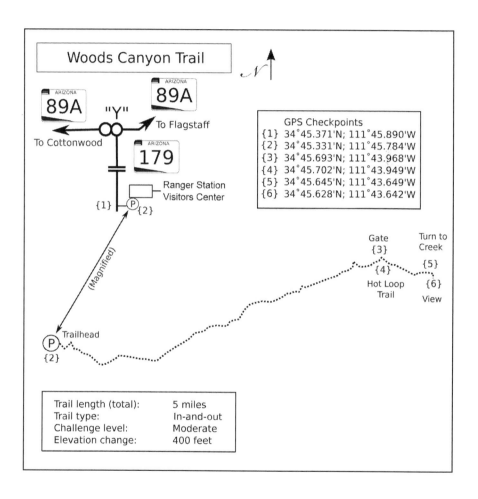

Hike GPS Waypoint Descriptions

Hike/GPS Checkpoint Description	Point	GPS Location
Airport Loop		
Parking for Bandit Trail	1	34 51.283 N; 111 48.015 W
Parking on Airport Road	2	34 51.345 N; 111 46.804 W
Intersect Tabletop Trail	3	34 50.773 N; 111 47.724 W
View Pyramid	4	34 50.448 N; 111 47.959 W
Intersect Bandit Trail	5	34 51.172 N; 111 47.718 W
Airport Vortex		
Parking on Airport Road	1	34 51.345 N; 111 46.804 W
Turn Left	2	34 51.330 N; 111 46.783 W
Turn Right	3	34 51.361 N; 111 46.780 W
Vortex	4	34 51.350 N; 111 46.741 W
Baldwin Trail		
Parking on Verde Valley School Road	1	34 49.309 N; 111 48.493 W
Sign Board	2	34 49.334 N; 111 48.438 W
Intersect Unmarked Trail	3	34 49.390 N; 111 48.176 W
Intersect Templeton Trail	4	34 49.347 N; 111 47.984 W
Across From Buddha Beach	5	34 49.401 N; 111 47.812 W
Snack Area 1	6	34 49.091 N; 111 48.043 W
Snack Area 2	7	34 48.844 N; 111 48.228 W
Intersect Unmarked Trail to VV School Rd	8	34 48.953 N; 111 48.476 W
Bear Mountain		
Parking on Boynton Pass Road	1	34 53.596 N; 111 51.945 W
Nice Photo	2	34 54.211 N; 111 52.497 W
Top of Bear Mountain	3	34 55.762 N; 111 53.607 W
Bear Sign		
Parking on FR 152	1	34 56.236 N; 111 47.678 W
Turn to Bear Sign Trail	2	34 56.723 N; 111 47.680 W
Intersect David Miller Trail	3	34 57.656 N; 111 49.054 W
Nice Photo	4	34 57.655 N; 111 49.179 W

Hike GPS Waypoint Descriptions

Hike/GPS Checkpoint Description	Point	GPS Location
Bell Rock Vortex		
Parking Area (North Bell Parking)	1	34 48.350 N; 111 46.009 W
Intersect Courthouse and Bell Rock Trails	2	34 48.176 N; 111 46.021 W
Signpost for Bell Trail	3	34 48.170 N; 111 45.996 W
Turn Right	4	34 48.135 N; 111 45.932 W
Meditation Perch	5	34 48.066 N; 111 45.953 W
Boynton Canyon and Vortex		
Parking Area	1	34 54.456 N; 111 50.928 W
Intersect Boynton Vista Trail	2	34 54.623 N; 111 50.987 W
Boynton Vortex	3	34 54.706 N; 111 50.885 W
Turn to Ruins	4	34 55.169 N; 111 51.233 W
Trail End	5	34 55.435 N; 111 52.697 W
Brins Mesa		
Parking Off Jordan Road	1	34 53.287 N; 111 46.098 W
Edge of Brins Mesa	2	34 54.022 N; 111 46.754 W
Intersect Soldier Pass Trail	3	34 54.302 N; 111 47.308 W
Parking on FR 152	4	34 55.008 N; 111 48.525 W
Broken Arrow		
Parking on Morgan Road	1	34 50.738 N; 111 45.424 W
Devil's Dining Room	2	34 50.321 N; 111 45.274 W
Turn to Submarine Rock	3	34 50.261 N; 111 45.226 W
Submarine Rock	4	34 50.245 N; 111 44.784 W
Chicken Point	5	34 49.794 N; 111 45.240 W
Cathedral Rock and Vortex		
Parking on Back O' Beyond Road	1	34 49.523 N; 111 47.303 W
Intersection of Cathedral Rock and Templeton	2	34 49.335 N; 111 47.369' W
Cathedral Rock Trail Continues Here	3	34 49.330 N; 111 47.400 W
Cathedral Rock Saddle and Vortex	4	34 49.154 N; 111 47.538 W

Hike GPS Waypoint Descriptions

Hike/GPS Checkpoint Description	Point	GPS Location
Chimney Rock Loop		
Parking Area	1	34 52.325 N; 111 48.735 W
Intersect Thunder Mountain and Chimney Rock Trails	2	34 52.405 N; 111 48.781 W
Intersect Andante Trail	3	34 52.659 N; 111 48.557 W
Thunder Mountain Trail Goes Right	4	34 52.718 N; 111 48.589 W
Fence Post	5	34 52.728 N; 111 48.741 W
Nice View	6	34 52.846 N; 111 48.658 W
Intersect Trail to Base of Chimneys	7	34 52.728 N; 111 48.773 W
Intersect Lizard Head Trail	8	34 52.768 N; 111 48.893 W
Continue Left	9	34 52.636 N; 111 48.936 W
Lower Chimney and Summit To Little Sugarloaf Trails	10	34 52.492 N; 111 48.935 W
Cibola Pass Trail		
Parking off Jordan Road	1	34 53.287 N; 111 46.098 W
Bear Left At Cibola/Brins Fork	2	34 53.281 N; 111 46.138 W
Turn Left Thru Fence Posts	3	34 53.283 N; 111 46.422 W
Meet Jordan Trail	4	34 53.188 N; 111 46.663 W
Devil's Kitchen	5	34 53.182 N; 111 46.944 W
Seven Sacred Pools	6	34 53.418 N; 111 47.149 W
Coffeepot Trail		
Parking Area	1	34 52.458 N; 111 47.793 W
Turn East (Right)	2	34 52.712 N; 111 47.843 W
Turn to Coffeepot Trail	3	34 52.793 N; 111 47.673 W
End of Trail (very steep)	4	34 53.024 N; 111 47.515 W
Cookstove to Harding Springs		
Parking at Cookstove Trail	1	35 00.877 N; 111 44.256 W
Trail Marker on Ponderosa tree	2	35 00.717 N; 111 43.997 W
Turn Away From Oak Creek Canyon	3	35 00.599 N; 111 44.009 W
Turn Right	4	35 00.593 N; 111 43.983 W
Turn Left	5	35 00.457 N; 111 43.828 W
Cross Wash 1	6	35 00.532 N; 111 43.705 W
Cross Wash 2	7	35 00.351 N; 111 43.590 W
Cross Wash 3, Turn Right Old Road Ahead	8	35 00.274 N; 111 43.577 W
Slight Right Off Road to Trail	9	35 00.231 N; 111 43.727 W
Intersect Harding Springs Trail	10	35 00.122 N; 111 43.881 W
Nice Overlook Area	11	35 00.099 N; 111 43.947 W
Harding Springs Trailhead	12	35 00.026 N; 111 44.226 W
Parking at Harding Springs Trail	13	35 00.039 N; 111 44.253 W

Hike GPS Waypoint Descriptions

Hike/GPS Checkpoint Description	Point	GPS Location
Courthouse Butte Loop		
North Bell Parking	1	34 48.350 N; 111 46.009 W
Intersect Llama Trail	2	34 48.332 N; 111 45.649 W
Muffin Rock	3	34 48.332 N; 111 45.012 W
Intersect Big Park Loop Trail	4	34 47.904 N; 111 44.891 W
Left Turn on Big Park Loop (Shortcut to South Parking)	5	34 47.851 N; 111 45.448 W
Intersect Courthouse Butte Loop Trail	6	34 47.860 N; 111 45.778 W
South Bell Parking	7	34 47.501 N; 111 45.699 W
Cowpies		
Parking on Schnebly Hill Road	1	34 52.318 N; 111 42.779 W
Vortex Area	2	34 52.411 N; 111 42.884 W
Turn to Cowpies	3	34 52.568 N; 111 42.914 W
Nice View	4	34 52.417 N; 111 43.193W
Nice View	5	34 52.321 N; 111 43.248 W
Devil's Bridge		
Parking on FR 152	1	34 54.172 N; 111 48.833 W
Turn to Overlook	2	34 53.897 N; 111 48.507 W
Overlook	3	34 53.911 N; 111 48.498 W
Trail Splits; Left Goes Under Arch, Straight to Arch	4	34 53.875 N; 111 48.497 W
Doe Mountain		
Parking on Boynton Pass Road	1	34 53.596 N; 111 51.945 W
Trail Up/Down	2	34 53.505 N; 111 51.643 W
Nice View 1	3	34 53.697 N; 111 51.568 W
Nice View 2	4	34 53.406 N; 111 51.572 W
Nice View 3	5	34 53.288 N; 111 51.862 W
Dry Creek		
Parking on FR 152	1	34 56.236 N; 111 47.678 W
Intersect Bear Sign Trail	2	34 56.723 N; 111 47.680 W
Turn Around Point	3	34 57.760 N; 111 47.526 W

Hike GPS Waypoint Descriptions

Hike/GPS Checkpoint Description	Point	GPS Location
Fay Canyon		
Parking on Boynton Pass Road	1	34 54.101 N; 111 51.450 W
Turn to Arch	2	34 54.507 N; 111 51.771 W
Arch	3	34 54.586 N; 111 51.673 W
Rock Slide	4	34 54.892 N; 111 52.082 W
Honanki		
Turn Right on Dry Creek	1	34 51.672 N; 111 48.948 W
Left on Boynton Canyon Road	2	34 53.915 N; 111 49.733 W
Left on Boynton Pass Road	3	34 54.376 N; 111 51.023 W
Right on FR 525	4	34 53.292 N; 111 54.379 W
Right at Fork	5	34 54.425 N; 111 54.748 W
Parking Area	6	34 56.193 N; 111 56.078 W
HS Canyon		
Parking on FR 152	1	34 55.797 N; 111 48.391 W
Turn to HS Canyon	2	34 56.299 N; 111 48.631 W
Huckaby		
Parking on Schnebly Hill Road	1	34 52.025 N; 111 44.946 W
View of Midgley Bridge	2	34 53.063 N; 111 44.580 W
Jim Thompson		
Parking off Jordan Road	1	34 53.287 N; 111 46.098 W
Jim Thompson Trailhead	2	34 53.324 N; 111 46.078 W
Intersect Jordan Trail	3	34 53.073 N; 111 45.883 W
View Midgley Bridge	4	34 53.357 N; 111 44.726 W
Intersect Wilson Canyon Trail	5	34 53.551 N; 111 44.507 W
Jordan Trail		
Parking off Jordan Road	1	34 53.287 N; 111 46.098 W
Another Jordan Trail Signpost	2	34 53.019 N; 111 49.040 W
Intersect Second Jordan Trail	3	34 52.983 N; 111 46.123 W
Intersect Cibola Trail	4	34 53.188 N; 111 46.663 W
Devil's Kitchen	5	34 53.182 N; 111 46.944 W
Seven Sacred Pools	6	34 53.418 N; 111 47.149 W

Hike GPS Waypoint Descriptions

Hike/GPS Checkpoint Description	Point	GPS Location
Kelly Canyon		
Turn off SR 89A	1	35 03.200 N; 111 43.960 W
Right Turn at Sign	2	35 03.517 N; 111 43.140 W
Park Here	3	35 03.501 N; 111 43.060 W
Go Downhill (east) to Pumphouse Wash	4	35 03.517 N; 111 43.020 W
Continue 500 feet east to where Trail Begins	5	35 03.531 N; 111 43.001 W
Intersect Trail 1; Turn Left, Go Down to Wash	6	35 03.688 N; 111 42.635 W
Right Turn to East Kelly Canyon	7	35 03.836 N; 111 42.320 W
East Kelly Canyon Stopping Point (you can continue)	8	35 03.938 N; 111 42.064 W
Ramp Over Downed Tree	9	35 03.989 N; 111 42.378 W
Intersect Trail 2	10	35 04.163 N; 111 42.335 W
Intersect Trail 3	11	35 04.697 N; 111 41.854 W
Intersect Forest Road 237	12	35 04.862 N; 111 41.820 W
Little Horse		
Parking Area	1	34 49.433 N; 111 46.555 W
Turn to Little Horse Trail	2	34 49.301 N; 111 46.308 W
Intersect Chapel Trail	3	34 49.705 N; 111 45.489 W
Chicken Point	4	34 49.794 N; 111 45.240 W
Llama Loop		
Parking Area (North Bell Parking)	1	34 48.350 N; 111 46.009 W
Left Turn	2	34 48.176 N; 111 46.015 W
Turn to Llama Trail	3	34 48.334 N; 111 45.651 W
Area of Depressions (pools)	4	34 48.574 N; 111 45.182 W
Turn Left	5	34 48.955 N; 111 45.660 W
Intersect Bell Rock Pathway	6	34 48.833 N; 111 45.908 W
Long Canyon		
Parking on Long Canyon Road	1	34 54.396 N; 111 49.476 W
Intersect Deadman Trail	2	34 55.040 N; 111 49.880 W
Turn Around Spot	3	34 56.175 N; 111 51.044 W
Lost Canyon		
Parking on FR 152	1	34 55.008 N; 111 48.525 W
Turn to Lost Canyon	2	34 55.007 N; 111 48.477 W
View Ruins	3	34 54.467 N; 111 48.163 W

Hike GPS Waypoint Descriptions

Hike/GPS Checkpoint Description	Point	GPS Location
Marg's Draw		
Parking on Morgan Road	1	34 50.738 N; 111 45.424 W
Parking on Sombart Lane	2	34 51.427 N; 111 45.677 W
Intersect Trail	3	34 51.399 N; 111 45.286 W
Parking on Schnebly Hill Road	4	34 52.025 N; 111 44.946 W
Mescal Mountain		
Parking on Long Canyon Road	1	34 54.396 N; 111 49.476 W
Turn to Mescal Mountain Trail	2	34 54.747 N; 111 49.844 W
Turn to Grandma's Cave	3	34 54.756 N; 111 50.147 W
Saddle	4	34 54.741 N; 111 50.249 W
Nice View	5	34 54.633 N; 111 50.230 W
Mitten Ridge		
Parking on Schnebly Hill Road	1	34 52.318 N; 111 42.779 W
Vortex Area	2	34 52.411 N; 111 42.884 W
Intersect Cowpies Trail	3	34 52.568 N; 111 42.914 W
Left Turn	4	34 52.637 N; 111 42.929 W
View Turnaround Point	5	34 52.349 N; 111 43.649 W
Munds Wagon		
Parking on Schnebly Hill Road	1	34 52.025 N; 111 44.946 W
Picnic Tables	2	34 52.098 N; 111 44.088 W
Turnaround Point	3	34 52.243 N; 111 43.289 W
Palatki		
Turn Right on Dry Creek	1	34 51.672 N; 111 48.948 W
Left on Boynton Canyon Road	2	34 53.915 N; 111 49.733 W
Left on Boynton Pass Road	3	34 54.376 N; 111 51.023 W
Right on FR 525	4	34 53.292 N; 111 54.379 W
Right at Fork	5	34 54.425 N; 111 54.748 W
Parking Area	6	34 54.963 N; 111 54.141 W

Hike GPS Waypoint Descriptions

Hike/GPS Checkpoint Description	Point	GPS Location
Pyramid		
Parking Area 1	1	34 50.202 N; 111 49.302 W
Turn Right	2	34 50.100 N; 111 49.218 W
Parking Area 2	3	34 50.096 N; 111 49.119 W
Thru Fence	4	34 50.002 N; 111 49.205 W
Steep Here	5	34 49.831 N; 111 49.200 W
Summit of Pyramid - View 1	6	34 49.878 N; 111 49.040 W
View 2	7	34 49.610 N; 111 49.316 W
Schuerman Mountain		
Parking Behind Red Rock High School	1	34 50.762 N; 111 49.716 W
Fork in Trail	2	34 50.458 N; 111 49.902 W
View of Cathedral Rock	3	34 50.283 N; 111 49.677 W
Secret Canyon		
Parking on FR 152	1	34 55.797 N; 111 48.391 W
HS Canyon Trailhead	2	34 56.299 N; 111 48.631 W
Intersect David Miller Trail	3	34 57.111 N; 111 49.211 W
Soldier Pass		
Parking Area	1	34 53.057 N; 111 47.028 W
Devil's Kitchen	2	34 53.182 N; 111 46.944 W
Seven Sacred Pools	3	34 53.418 N; 111 47.149 W
View Arches	4	34 53.865 N; 111 47.269 W
Intersect Brins Mesa Trail	5	34 54.302 N; 111 47.308 W
Sterling Pass to Vultee Arch		
Park on SR 89A	1	34 56.185 N; 111 44.829 W
Saddle	2	34 56.066 N; 111 45.579 W
Sign for Vultee Arch	3	34 56.384 N; 111 46.148 W
Parking on FR 152	4	34 56.236 N; 111 47.678 W
Sugarloaf		
Parking Area	1	34 52.459 N; 111 47.780 W
Turn East (Right)	2	34 52.712 N; 111 47.843 W
Turn to Sugarloaf Peak	3	34 52.735 N; 111 47.689 W
Sugarloaf Peak	4	34 52.583 N; 111 47.654 W

Hike GPS Waypoint Descriptions

Hike/GPS Checkpoint Description	Point	GPS Location
Templeton		
Parking on Back O' Beyond Road	1	34 49.523 N; 111 47.303 W
Intersection of Cathedral Rock and Templeton	2	34 49.335 N; 111 47.369 W
Intersection of Templeton and HT Trails	3	34 48.973 N; 111 46.580 W
Intersect SR 179	4	34 49.159 N; 111 46.430 W
Turkey Creek/House Mountain		
Turn Off Verde Valley School Road	1	34 48.736 N; 111 48.540 W
Trailhead	2	34 48.571 N; 111 49.070 W
Turn Right	3	34 48.340 N; 111 49.067 W
First Ridge	4	34 47.677 N; 111 50.280 W
Marker	5	34 47.368 N; 111 50.338 W
Top of House Mountain	6	34 46.833 N; 111 49.936 W
V Bar V Petroglyph Site		
Turn off FR 618	1	34 39.981 N; 111 42.802 W
Parking Area	2	34 39.986 N; 111 42.942 W
Visitor Center	3	34 39.974 N; 111 43.005 W
Rock Art	4	34 39.625 N; 111 43.136 W
Vultee Arch		
Parking on FR 152	1	34 56.236 N; 111 47.678 W
Sign for Vultee Arch	2	34 56.384 N; 111 46.148 W
Vultee Arch	3	34 56.500 N; 111 46.123 W
Weir Trail		
Parking Area Off FR 618	1	34 40.457 N; 111 42.795 W
Intersect White Mesa Trail	2	34 40.831 N; 111 41.136 W
Intersect Apache Maid Trail	3	34 40.700 N; 111 40.692 W
Intersect Bell Trail	4	34 40.605 N; 111 40.577 W
Weir	5	34 40.498 N; 111 40.334 W

Hike GPS Waypoint Descriptions

Hike/GPS Checkpoint Description	Point	GPS Location
West Fork		
Parking on SR 89A	1	34 59.446 N; 111 44.570 W
Mayhew's Lodge	2	34 59.301 N; 111 44.753 W
First Creek Crossing	3	34 59.301 N; 111 44.879 W
Nice Place For a Snack	4	34 59.772 N; 111 44.942 W
Huge Overhang (Look Below)	5	35 00.154 N; 111 45.603 W
Trail on Left Goes to Cave	6	35 00.158 N; 111 45.768 W
End of Trail (Need to Wade to Go Further)	7	35 00.106 N; 111 46.017 W
Wilson Canyon		
Parking on SR 89A	1	34 53.143 N; 111 44.501 W
Intersect Wilson Mountain South Trail	2	34 53.487 N; 111 44.455 W
Intersect Jim Thompson Trail	3	34 53.551 N; 111 44.507 W
Turn Around Point	4	34 54.023 N; 111 44.901 W
Wilson Mountain South Trail		
Parking on SR 89A	1	34 53.143 N; 111 44.501 W
Right Turn	2	34 53.651 N; 111 44.537 W
Reach First Bench	3	34 54.480 N; 111 44.414 W
Top of Wilson Mountain	4	34 55.304 N; 111 45.500 W
Woods Canyon		
Turn Off SR 179	1	34 45.371 N; 111 45.890 W
Parking Area	2	34 45.331 N; 111 45.784 W
Gate	3	34 45.693 N; 111 43.968 W
Intersect Hot Loop Trail	4	34 45.702 N; 111 43.949 W
Turn to Creek	5	34 45.645 N; 111 43.649 W
View of Creek	6	34 45.628 N; 111 43.642 W

Hikes Rated by Level of Difficulty

Easy

Airport Vortex
Coffeepot Trail
Cowpies Trail
Honanki Indian Ruins
Palatki Indian Ruins
V Bar V

Easy to Moderate

Airport Loop Trail
Bell Rock Trail
Dry Creek Trail
Fay Canyon Trail
Jordan Trail
Kelly Canyon Trail
Llama Trail
Marg's Draw Trail
Vultee Arch Trail

Moderate

Baldwin Trail
Bear Sign Trail
Boynton Canyon Trail
Brins Mesa Trail
Broken Arrow Trail
Chimney Rock Trail
Cibola Pass Trail
Courthouse Loop Trail
Devil's Bridge Trail
Doe Mountain Trail
HS Canyon Trail

Hikes Rated by Level of Difficulty

<u>Moderate</u>

Huckaby Trail
Jim Thompson Trail
Little Horse Trail
Long Canyon Trail
Lost Canyon Trail
Mescal Mountain Trail
Mitten Ridge Trail
Munds Wagon Trail
Pyramid Trail
Schuerman Mountain Trail
Secret Canyon Trail
Soldier Pass Trail
Sugarloaf Trail
Templeton Trail
Weir Trail
West Fork Trail
Wilson Canyon Trail
Woods Canyon Trail

<u>Hard</u>

Bear Mountain Trail
Cathedral Rock Trail
Cookstove/Harding Sprngs
Sterling Pass/Vultee Arch
Turkey Creek/House Mt.
Wilson Mountain Trail

Hikes By Feature

Hikes to/Near Arches

Devil's Bridge (pg. 46)
Fay Canyon (pg. 52)
Soldier Pass (pg. 90)
Vultee Arch (pg.102)

Indian Ruin Hikes

Boynton Canyon (pg.26)
Honanki Indian Ruins (pg.54)
Lost Canyon (pg. 72)
Mescal Mountain (pg. 76)
Palatki Indian Ruins (pg. 82)
V Bar V Petroglyph Site (pg. 100)

Vortex Hikes

Airport Vortex (pg. 16)
Bell Rock (pg. 24)
Boynton Canyon (Vista) (pg.26)
Cathedral Rock (pg. 32)
Cowpies (pg. 44)

Water Hikes

Baldwin (pg. 18)
Huckaby (pg. 58)
Munds Wagon - spring
   runoff only (pg. 80)
Templeton (pg. 96)
Weir (pg. 104)
West Fork (pg. 106)
Woods Canyon (pg. 112)

Favorite Hikes

There are many hiking trails in and around Sedona. We chose our 50 favorite hikes for this guidebook. But even within that group we have our favorites, the best of the best. And they are (in alphabetical order):

Baldwin
Bear Mountain
Boynton Canyon
Brins Mesa
Devil's Bridge
Doe Mountain
Fay Canyon
Little Horse
Llama Loop
Secret Canyon
West Fork

Scenic Drives

Here are several scenic drives around the Sedona area where you can take some excellent photographs of the red rock formations. All of the roads mentioned below are paved, with the exception of Schnebly Hill Road, which is paved only for the first mile.

Airport Overlook

Atop Airport Mesa is a scenic overlook, which provides magnificent views of Coffeepot Rock, Thunder Mountain, Sugarloaf and Chimney Rock. Looking west across the Verde Valley, you'll see the Black Hills; on a clear day you can even see the "J" above Jerome, Arizona.

From the "Y" roundabout (the intersection of State Route 89A and State Route 179), drive west toward Cottonwood on SR 89A for 1 mile and turn then left on Airport Road. Proceed up Airport Road for 1.1 miles to the scenic overlook on your right. The free parking area is on your left at GPS coordinates: 34° 51.178' N; 111° 47.390' W. Once you have parked, cross the road and enjoy the view. Donations are accepted to help maintain the overlook.

Sedona's Namesake (Sedona Schnebly)

The grave of Sedona Schnebly, for whom the town is named is located off Airport Road. Drive up Airport Road a short distance and turn right at the Elk's Club sign, just beyond the U Haul trailer rental facility. Park in front of the "Cook's Cedar Glade Cemetery" arch on your right and proceed north about 75 paces to GPS coordinates 34° 51.685' N; 111° 46.866' W. Inside the low wall you'll find the grave of Sedona Schnebly (1877- 1950).

Bell Rock/Courthouse Butte/Lee Mountain

Bell Rock is one of the most recognizable rock formations in Sedona. And Courthouse Butte, along with Lee Mountain, are sights many visitors first see when they arrive in Sedona driving north on State Route 179. There are two parking areas at Bell Rock, one to the north and one to the south. You can take photographs of Bell Rock, Courthouse Butte and Lee Mountain any time of day because from the south side of Bell Rock, the sun will be behind you.

From the "Y" (the intersection of State Route 89A and State Route 179), travel south on State Route 179 for about 8 miles. First you'll see the north parking area on your left. Proceed on SR 179 for another 1 mile and then turn into the south parking area. From here you'll have great views of the rock formations.

Chapel of the Holy Cross

This isn't a scenic drive in the true sense, but the Chapel of the Holy Cross is a local landmark and a must-see. It was opened in 1956 and serves as a place to meditate and enjoy the beauty that is Sedona.

From the "Y" roundabout (the intersection of State Route 89A and State Route 179), proceed south on SR 179 for 2.8 miles and then drive 270 degrees (3/4 of the way) around the Chapel Road roundabout. Proceed east on Chapel Road to the end. The Chapel has a gift shop located in the lower level. Take time to observe the fine views from the Chapel. There is no charge to park or enter the Chapel, but donations are accepted.

Dry Creek Road

The drive out Dry Creek Road provides outstanding views of the red rocks of Secret Mountain Wilderness. The road is paved so any vehicle can make the drive.

From the "Y" roundabout (the intersection of State Route 89A and State Route 179), drive west toward Cottonwood on SR 89A for 3 miles. Turn right on Dry Creek Road (where speed limits are strictly enforced). Stay on Dry Creek to a stop sign (about 3 miles) and then turn left on Boynton Pass Road. Proceed about 1.5 miles to a stop sign. Turn right to go 0.2 mile to the Enchantment Resort; turn left and then you can drive the 2 mile paved stretch of Boynton Pass Road.

Oak Creek Canyon

The drive up Oak Creek Canyon is a world-famous route that always delights. You begin in Sedona and drive toward Flagstaff to a Scenic View Area. As you follow along the path cut by Oak Creek over millions of years, the views and solitude are beautiful. Cell phone use is limited in Oak Creek Canyon. You'll go up in elevation from about 4500 feet (Sedona) to 6400 feet (at the Scenic View Area).

From the "Y" roundabout (the intersection of State Route 89A and State Route 179), proceed north on SR 89A through Uptown Sedona.

As you proceed, you'll probably want to pull over and take photographs. Be sure you pull off the road far enough to let vehicles pass by. Drive up Oak Creek Canyon for 16 miles and turn right into the Scenic View Area. If you drove up Oak Creek Canyon, ask someone else to drive back to Sedona so you can enjoy the views.

Schnebly Hill Road

We suggest you have a high-clearance vehicle for this drive. Schnebly Hill Road is paved for the first 1 mile and the views don't begin until the very rough unpaved portion of the road. In wet weather, the gate at the end of the pavement is sometimes closed because of road conditions. Also, in winter Schnebly Hill Road is closed about 4.3 miles in at the "Merry-Go-Round." If the gate is open, proceed on for another 1.7 miles to the Schnebly Hill Vista at GPS coordinates: 34° 53.385' N; 111° 42.194' W for some amazing views. If you stop along the road, be sure to pull your vehicle far enough off the road to let other vehicles by.

From the "Y" roundabout (the intersection of State Route 89A and State Route 179), go south on SR 179 about 0.3 mile to the Schnebly Hill Roundabout and then drive 270 degrees (3/4 of the way) around to Schnebly Hill Road. Proceed 1 mile on paved road and then continue on the unpaved section of Schnebly Hill Road. If the road is not closed, you can drive all the way to Interstate 17, but after about 6 miles, there are minimal views.

Upper Red Rock Loop Road

The drive on the Upper Red Rock Loop Road provides outstanding views of Cathedral Rock, with Courthouse Butte and Bell Rock in the distance. It is the road to Crescent Moon Ranch/Red Rock Crossing, where you can stroll along the banks of Oak Creek and take photographs of Cathedral Rock with Oak Creek in the foreground, one of the most recognized photographic settings in Sedona.

From the "Y" (the intersection of State Route 89A and State Route 179), drive west on SR 89A for 4.25 miles and then turn left on the Upper Red Rock Loop Road. Follow the Upper Loop Road for about 1.9 miles for the best views. If you want to continue to Crescent Moon Ranch/Red Rock Crossing, turn left on Chavez Ranch Road and then follow it for about 1 mile to the end until you reach the entrance gate.

How to Talk Like a Local

Here's some local vocabulary for the trail and the drive to the trailhead. Five minutes of study and you'll sound like you've been hiking in Sedona for years.

Arizona Pinstripes: Most Arizona vegetation has needles and thorns, and many of the roads have brush and tree branches encroaching. You'll want to watch as you drive those roads to make sure your vehicle doesn't get too close to that vegetation, or you'll end up with nice deep scratches (pinstripes) in the paint.

Cairn: A trail marker constructed of stacked rocks. Many are small, but some may be waist-high and held together by a wire basket.

Carousel: Most of the wonderful rock formations around Sedona have self-explanatory names, but two that don't are the "Carousel" or "Merry-Go-Round" and the "Fin" (see pictures of each below each of their descriptions). The Carousel sits in the center of a ring of Fort Apache limestone, about 4 miles up Schnebly Hill Road. If your vehicle can handle this primitive road, the Carousel is a great destination for outstanding views.

Fin: The Fin's name is obvious to anyone who has seen the dorsal fin of a large fish. It is located close to the center of town, and great views of it can be had from the Jim Thompson Trail.

Hoodoo: A rock spire. There are plenty of these to admire when you're hiking in the Sedona area; this one sits near the Baldwin Trail.

Javelina (ha – veh – LEE – nah): Sometimes called "pigs" for short, javelinas are actually collared peccaries, a species that migrated up from central America relatively recently. If you encounter javelinas on the trail, don't worry; they'll typically try to avoid you. But don't make a javelina feel cornered, don't try to feed it, and *never* get near a mother and baby javelina. If you hike with a dog, keep it leashed. "Javelina," or javelin, refers to the specie's razor-sharp canine teeth. The photo below was taken with a long lens.

Rock Art: Fairly common in the Sedona area, these Native American images can date from around 10,000 BC to the late 19th century. There are two primary types: petroglyphs (below left), which were chipped or scratched into the surface of the rock (such as found at the V-Bar-V site), and pictographs (below right), which were painted on the surface using vegetable and mineral colors.

Slickrock: Any large slab of red sandstone. It may be slick when wet or icy, but usually gives the hiker good footing when dry. The slickrock pictured below is part of the Cow Pies hike.

Social Trails: Unofficial, unmarked trails created by hikers, often as a short-cut. Staying on the established trails is safer, and protects the fragile surrounding vegetation.

Index

Index

Made in the USA
Charleston, SC
30 August 2010